The ABC of Research Methods: Notes for Graduate Students

Ibrahim Farah
Hashim Shuria
Himish Mahmoud

1445/2024

LOOH PRESS LTD.
Copyright © Ibrahim Farah, Hashim Shuria, Himish Mahmoud, 2024
First Edition, First Print 2021
Second Edition, First Print June 2024

All rights reserved.
No part of this publication may be reproduced, stored in any retrieval system, or transmitted in any form or by any means, including photocopying, recording, or other electronic or mechanical methods, without the prior written permission of the publisher, except in the case of brief quotations embodied in critical reviews and certain other noncommercial uses permitted by copyright law.

For permission and requests, write to the publisher or the author, at the address below.

PRINTED & DISTRIBUTED BY
Looh Press Ltd.
56 Lethbridge Close
Leicester, England. UK
www.LoohPress.com
LoohPress@gmail.com

CORRESPONDING AUTHOR:
farahiq2002@yahoo.com

A catalogue record of this title is available from the British Library.

COVER DESIGN & TYPESET
Kusmin (Looh Press)

ISBN
978-1-912411-68-9   Paperback

Contents

Acronyms ix
Acknowledgements xi
Preface xiii
Foreword xvii

1. **An Introductory Overview** 1
   The Meaning and Objectives of Research 1
   Types and Approaches of Research 2
   Other Types of Research 4
   Research Approaches 7
   Significance of Research 8
   The Research Process 10
   Formulating the Research Problem 11
   Reviewing 12
   Developing the Hypotheses 12
   Research Design 13
   Sampling 14
   Data Collection 15
   Project Execution 15
   Data Analysis 15
   Criteria for Good Research 16
   Limitation of Research Methods 17
   End of Chapter 1 Quiz 19

2. **Social Science and Research Methods: The History** 21
   Introduction 21
   The Development of Social Sciences as a Scientific Discipline: An Overview 21
   Historical Transformation of Social Science Research Methodology 23
   Conclusions 25
   End of Chapter 2 Quiz 26

3. **Epistemological Aspects of Research** 27
   Introduction.. 27
   Assumptions of Positivism 32
   Application in Research 33
   Post-positivism 34
   Conclusions 35
   End of Chapter 3 Quiz 36

4. **Introduction to Quantitative Research**..37
   Introduction... 37
   What is Quantitative Research? 37
   Foundations of Quantitative Research Methods 39
   When Do We Use Quantitative Methods? 39
   Types of Quantitative Research 40
   Designing Non-experimental Studies (Survey) 41
   Conclusions 43
   End of Chapter 4 Quiz 44

5. **Introduction to Qualitative Research** 45
   Introduction... 45
   Qualitative Research Designs 46
   Theory and Research Strategies 47
   Table 1.0: Qualitative Research Strategy 47
   Convenience Samples 49
   Purposive Sampling 50
   Snowball Sampling.. 50
   Quota Samples 50
   When to Use Qualitative Research: 51
   What, how, and why?.. 51
   The Functions of Different Qualitative Methods 52
   Naturally occurring data... 52
   Generated data 53
   Mixing qualitative approaches.. 54
   Conclusions 54
   End of Chapter 5 Quiz 55

6. **Introduction to Mixed Methods Research**..57
   Introduction... 57
   Defining Mixed Methods Research 57
   Why Mixed Methods?.. 58
   Mixed Methods Approach: Strategies of Inquiry............................. 59
   Sequential Procedures... 59
   Concurrent Procedures 60

    Transformative Procedures 61
    Strengths and Weaknesses of Mixed Method Research 61
    Strengths: 62
    Weaknesses 62
    Conclusions 63
    End of Chapter 6 Quiz 64

7. Research Design and Management 65
    Introduction 65
    Why Research Design? 66
    Features of a Good Research Design 67
    Different Research Designs 70
    Research Design—Exploratory Research Studies 70
    Research Design— Descriptive and Diagnostic Research Studies 70
    Research Design—Hypothesis-testing Research Studies 71
    Conclusions 71
    End of Chapter 7 Quiz 72

8. Data Collection Methods 73
    Introduction 73
    Raw Data 73
    Defining Variables 74
    Quantitative Data 75
    Qualitative Data 75
    Univariate Data 75
    Bivariate Data 76
    Multivariate Data 76
    Sources of Data 76
    Data Collection Methods for Quantitative Research 76
    Data Measurements 76
    Data Collection Techniques 78
    Data Collection Methods for Quantitative Research 78
    Survey Methods 78
    The Experimental Method 80
    Data Collection Techniques for Qualitative Research 82
    In-Depth Interviewing 82
    Why Use In-depth Interviews? 83
    Focus Group Discussions (FGDs) 83
    Strengths of Focus Groups versus In-depth Interviews 84
    The Observation Method 85
    Dimensions of Observation 85
    Preparing for Observation 86

    How to Conduct an Observational Study 87
    Conclusions 87
    End of Chapter 8 Quiz 88

9. Data Analysis and Interpretation 89
    Introduction 89
    Data Processing and Presentation 90
    Quantitative Data Analysis 90
    Descriptive Statistics 91
    Summary of Central Tendencies and Variability 92
    Inferential Statistics 93
    Qualitative Data Analysis 95
    Table 1. Possible Qualitative Analyses for Research 96
    Use of Computer-Assisted Qualitative Data Analysis Software 100
    Presenting the Data 101
    End of Chapter 9 Quiz 102
    Conclusions 102

10. Research Proposal Writing 103
    Introduction 103
    Types of Research 104
    Criteria for Good Research 105
    Proposal Writing 105
    The Structure of a Research Proposal 106
    Conclusions 111
    End of Chapter 10 Quiz 112

11. Research Ethics 113
    Introduction 113
    Ethical Principles of Social Research Methods 114
    Professional Codes of Ethics 115
    Codes and Policies for Research Ethics 117
    Plagiarism 119
    Referencing 119
    Style Guide 120
    Research Ethics and Law 122
    Conclusions 122
    End of Chapter 11 Quiz 123
    Pre-Exam Review 123

Annex 1 125

Bibliography 131

Acronyms

ABC	The alphabet; the basics
AIS	Association of Information Systems
ALTEM	Adult Learning Techniques and Methodologies
ANOVA	Analysis of Variance
APA	American Psychological Association
CAQDAS	Computer-Assisted Qualitative Data Analysis Software
CMS	Chicago Manual of Style
DOIs	Digital Object Identifiers
DRC	Democratic Republic of Congo
FGDs	Focus Group Discussions
JPN	Justice & Peace Network
M&E	Monitoring & Evaluation
MLA	Modern Language Association
PhD	Doctor of Philosophy
QUAL	Qualitative
QUAN	Quantitative

RCC	Rationality, Creativity and Critical-thinking
SAS	Statistical Analysis System
SMART	Specific, Measurable, Achievable, Realistic and Time-bound
SPSS	Statistical Package for Social Sciences
ToT	Training of Trainers
URLs	Uniform Resource Locators

Acknowledgements

First of all, we thank Allah (SWT) for everything!

In *The ABC of Research Methods: Notes for Graduate Students*, we share a few ideas derived from countless academics, researchers and policy-makers throughout the world. These are the people who, through research, struggle every day to generate new knowledge and at the same time contribute to the existing body of knowledge and to ongoing policy debates touching the everyday lives of millions of people. This book in every way captures their ideas, hopes and aspirations as it aims to help equip graduate students – and from the basics – with the necessary ability to let them conceptualize, conduct research and find knowledge, and then constructively apply the findings.

As a result, and as we used our knowledge to put this together, our studies, lecture seminars to students, and library resources were the test-grounds for our ideas to put this manuscript together. This brings in a number of universities and other educational donor institutions in mind, for which we are forever grateful. From the University of Nairobi (Nairobi-Kenya), to the German Academic Exchange Service (DAAD/ Nairobi-Kenya), to SIMAD University (Mogadishu-Somalia), to the University of East Africa (Garowe- Somalia), to the University of Southern Somalia (Baidoa-Somalia), City University (Mogadishu- Somalia), to Jazeera University (Mogadishu- Somalia), to Gedo International University (B/hawa-Somalia) and to the many other universities, research institutes and other policy forums which we have visited to discuss research methods and immensely benefited from their comments and critique, we thank them all and we are deeply grateful. We also thank Akademiyaha Soomaalida and ResearchCare Africa for supporting this book project and helping us realize its publication.

Our families come first, second and last. A million thanks to them all, let alone everything else but more, for their valuable time and patience. By Allah's grace, they have been central to this book project AND without their moral support we would have not had this book out.

A number of ideas included in this book are not referenced. Through interactive discussions, they were contributed by fellow academics, researchers, policy-makers and other fellow scholars as part of our ongoing research for this 3-year book project on the basics of research methods. You all challenged us in order to make us understand that "everybody knows something but nobody knows everything" and with this philosophy, we had to share the little we thought we knew as we learnt from everybody through this book project. To all, we are deeply – and forever – grateful for what you have taught us about the meaning and importance of research; be it academic, policy, or otherwise.

Ibrahim Farah
Hashim Shuria
Himish Mahmoud
London/Mogadishu: June 2024

Preface

It is the desire of all social science-based graduate programmes to produce students whose competencies span three important dimensions. The first dimension is an in-depth theoretical understanding of social phenomena. The second dimension is the ability to formulate and conduct credible research on the social phenomena. The third dimension is, on the one hand, the ability to interpret research findings to explain the social phenomena thus contributing to the advancement of knowledge, and on the other hand, ability to propose evidence-based policy solutions to social problems facing humanity through research, and thereafter through development and innovation. The first dimension is usually built from undergraduate training and work experience. This also lays the foundation for the second dimension—the deeper theoretical understanding of social phenomena, sharpened through more specialized training in graduate school.

The objective of this publication: *"The ABC of Research Methods: Notes for Graduate Students"* is to help graduate students mold the second and third dimensions mentioned above; the ability to conceptualize and conduct research and then apply it. It takes cognizance of the futility of theoretical knowledge of social phenomena if graduate students are incapable of conceptualizing and conducting research in pursuit of explanations or policy solutions to the social problems. Using a simple and easy-to-understand language and style, this publication compiles the foundations, basic principles and steps of research in eleven chapters.

Chapter one provides an introductory overview of research and its conceptual issues. The second chapter delves into the historical aspects of research, explaining the evolution of social studies into science, just as the natural sciences have been methodologically studied while chapter three focuses on the epistemological underpinnings of research by reviewing the major philosophical approaches of research. Chapter four, five and six delve into the methodology of research; quantitative, qualitative and mixed methods research respectively. Chapter seven, eight and nine address research design, data collection and analysis, respectively. Chapter ten focuses on proposal writing, an integral component of graduate students' work that encompasses all aspects from chapter one to chapter nine of this publication. The last chapter deals with ethics of research, highlighting ethical principles governing researchers, their relationships with research subjects, colleagues and due credit to previously done research and other academic works.

This book is intended to be used as an instructional resource for graduate students to support not only their understanding of research but also the capability to conceptualize and conduct credible research. It has been done in an easy style, using a deliberately simplified language in order to achieve this objective. The chapters and concepts are logically organized, from mundane to complex in order to facilitate a systematic learning of the nuances and contours of research, with illustrative charts and tables where appropriate.

Like any other scholarly work, this book was not developed without challenges. This is based on the fact that all endeavours to develop instructional materials on research usually face the practical lack of room for novelty. This is essentially because of the universality of research principles. Nonetheless, the strength of this publication lies in its authors' understanding of the instructional needs of the target graduate students in post-conflict societies, for example; Somalia, South Sudan and the Democratic Republic of Congo (DRC), wherein also lies its novelty, the ability to tailor the material to be used to teach research in a context where, due to known socio- economic and political circumstances, there is lack of such materials.

While the manuscript does not provide basic illustrative statistical examples typical of instructional materials on research, it is, however, the understanding of the authors that a publication like this would typically lay the foundation for understanding of research. After reading this book, graduate students will need a stand-alone advanced course on research methods. This can either be the next phase of a research methods series or a separate book project with which the target audience—Somalia's Higher Learning Institutions may think of engaging next. For illustrative purposes, it is expected of the lecturers teaching courses on research methods to cover the necessary mathematical calculations.

Finally, as the authors of this book, we are of the strong view that the publication of a book on research methods, no matter how basic, that is; *The ABC of Research Methods: Notes for Graduate Students*, for today's Somalia is not only timely but also very beneficial. It is believed that it will greatly contribute to the improvement of quality of education through the basics of research methods at a time when Somalia's higher learning institutions are equally struggling with (over three-decade long) peace-building and state-building efforts; hence a bold initiative to make whatever contribution one can make to the recreation of a new Somalia, and new Africa through quality education.

Foreword

Good quality education is a rare commodity in the contemporary Somalia, which places research methodology, as an area of study, among disciplines most sought after, but much less domesticated in the academic community in the country. The gaps and flaws hindering the learner from accessing the dark alleys that lay in the sub-genres of research methodology have extended wider. Consequently, the lack of consideration in problematizing the matter in order to master the discipline has remained an enduring epidemic in the country's academic arena and therefore a persistent issue, though often skipping our scholarly attention. However, this revised edition, *The ABC of Research Methods: Notes for Graduate Students,* provides a symptom of hope as it is a right step forward that pioneers to address the perplexity that has confronted Somali students eager to digest the subject but helpless in accessing literature more relevantly designed to address the needs of the local context.

This volume is exquisitely tailored to address a major gap in the quality of Somali higher education. It opens a learning opportunity whose aim is to support ambitious students as well as expert professionals cope with the tricky corners in the discipline. *The ABC of Research Methods: Notes for Graduate Students* is keenly designed to respond to the need for research education in the national milieu while also aspiring to attract extensive readership from the regional, continental and global context. The authors of the book have considered several factors to the advantage of the student and expert with a basic intent of boosting student morale. For quality-oriented higher learning institutions, this is the kind of course reader which facilitates mentoring of students as novice researchers early enough in their studies so that the very basics, 'the ABC of research methods,' is mastered and graduate students are prepared enough to occupy positions as researchers or develop robust leadership characteristics in the research field. From these viewpoints, this revised edition serves the entire higher education industry and the world of professional research.

A unique volume of its kind, *The ABC of Research Methods: Notes for Graduate Students* is a much more simplified version that appeals to every student with a desire for a quick grasp of textual as well as conceptual substance of research education without much struggle with verbosity and hard-nut linguistic jargons, while not undermining the use of relevant, subject-related terms and terminologies. With its magnitude of intellectual corpus covering extensive areas of the subject Research Methodology, the book brings an unmatched, unparalleled sophistication into the existing disciplinary literature in the wider Horn of Africa, the entire East Africa region, the continent and the global arena. It is indeed a prompt intellectual contribution that substantively complements preceding works such as *Research Methods: Qualitative and Quantitative Approaches* by Mugenda and Mugenda (2003), Mary Ngechu's (2002) *Understanding Research Process and Methods: An Introduction*, and Peter Wasamba's more recent publication, of 2015, focusing on field-based oral research methods for the literary world and entitled *Contemporary Oral Literature Fieldwork: A Researcher's Guide*.

The ABC of Research Methods: Notes for Graduate Students is a well-conceived, superbly constructed volume that sets the benchmark for young researchers keen to learn and understand the in-depth processes involved in academic, policy and professional research. As a ready-made research toolkit, the book is written to help university students gain a nuanced cutting-edge knowledge that enables them to comfortably access the distinct theories, processes, and paradigms of the research method. The book, therefore, is aimed at enriching the theoretical knowledge base of the students while at the same time guiding them to embark on practical application through experiential learning that balances theory with practice.

What makes this revised edition of *The ABC of Research Methods: Notes for Graduate Students* more appealing to the reader is the combination of the depth of its richness and conciseness with which that resourcefulness is presented. Unlike other books, reading this tailor-made volume does not consume time as it is a good weekend read—it's a book which takes very short time for an average reader to finish it. The eleven chapters of the book are considerately arranged and carefully sequenced in such a way that the student unfamiliar with the research method process as well as the expert are guided from general introductory discussion of the theory of research to the details of the broader themes and sub-themes that allows the reader to hold the material corpus together. From early debates to contemporary discussions, this revised edition of *The ABC of Research Methods: Notes for Graduate Students* provides both a diagnostic aspect of theory and an empirical focus engendered toward practical substance, assisting the student to retain gained knowledge with end-chapter quizzes, a pre-exam review, a ToT package and a non-exhaustive reference list that makes the book a more easily accessible tool-kit. Congratulations to Prof. Farah and his colleagues!

The ABC of Research Methods: Notes for Graduate Students is a timely contribution that addresses needed issues in research methodology as a discipline of study while fulfilling all the necessities of an intellectual capacity building compendium for undergraduate, graduate as well as expert scholars. Enjoy it!

Professor Dr. Mohamed A. Eno
Executive President- University of Southern Somalia (Baidoa)

AN INTRODUCTORY OVERVIEW

> *"All progress is born of inquiry. Doubt is often better than overconfidence, for it leads to inquiry, and inquiry leads to invention."*
>
> — **Hudson Maxim (1853-1927)**

The Meaning and Objectives of Research

According to Kothari (2004:1), "Research in common parlance refers to a search for knowledge." It is the scientific and systematic search for pertinent information on a specific topic or simply, an art of scientific investigation (Nachmias and Nachmias, 1992). According to Clifford (1924), "Research comprises defining and redefining problems, formulating hypothesis or suggested solutions; collecting, organising and evaluating data; making deductions and reaching conclusions; and at last, carefully testing the conclusions to determine whether they fit the formulating hypothesis."

The purpose of research is to discover answers to questions through the application of scientific procedures. The main aim of research is to find out the truth which is hidden and which has not been discovered yet. Though each research study has its own specific purpose, we may think of research objectives as:

a). To gain familiarity with a phenomenon or to achieve new insights into it (studies with this object in view are termed as *exploratory* or *formulative* research studies),

b). To accurately portray the characteristics of a particular individual, situation or group (studies with this object in view are known as *descriptive* research studies),

c). To determine the frequency with which a phenomenon occurs or with which it is associated with something else (studies with this object in view are known as *diagnostic* research studies),

d). To test a hypothesis of a causal relationship between variables (such studies are known as *hypothesis-testing* research studies), and finally

e). To answer research questions.

Types and Approaches of Research

Mishra and Alok (2012) outline basic types of research as follows:

a) *Descriptive vs Analytical:* Descriptive research consists of surveys and fact-finding endeavours aimed at providing and describing a phenomenon as it exists. In social science and business research, quite often the term *ex post facto* research is used for descriptive research studies to imply the fact that in such an endeavour, the researcher has no control over the variables because the events have occurred prior to the researcher's current observation. Thus, such research can only report what has happened or what is happening.

According to Mishra and Alok (2012), most *ex post facto* research projects are used for descriptive studies in which the researcher seeks to measure items such as; frequency of shopping, preferences of people or similar data. Such studies may also attempt to investigate causality regardless of the disadvantage over variables already stated above.

b) *Applied vs Fundamental*: Research is broadly categorized as either *applied* (action) research or *fundamental* (basic or pure) research. Applied research aims at finding a solution for an immediate problem facing a society or an industrial, or a business organisation, whereas fundamental research is mainly concerned with generalisations and formulation of theory. Applied research, which is also called practitioner research, may be exemplified when a corporate organization commissions a study to find out acceptability of their product or when a government conducts a study to understand why a group of people behaves in a certain undesirable way and how to mitigate the behaviour. It seeks furtherance of knowledge to solve the problem existing within the boundary of that particular corporation or department.

The process of research that involves gathering knowledge for its own sake is termed *'pure'* or *'basic'* research. Research concerning some natural phenomenon or relating to pure mathematics are examples of fundamental research. Similarly, research studies concerning human behaviour carried out with a view to make generalisations about human behaviour are also examples of fundamental research. However, research aimed at certain conclusions (say, a solution) facing a concrete social or business problem is an example of applied research and is usually carried out by experts working in the corporation.

c) *Quantitative vs Qualitative:* Quantitative research is premised on the measurement of *quantity* or amount mathematically. It is applicable to phenomena that can be expressed in terms of quantity. Qualitative research, on the other hand, is concerned with *qualitative* phenomena, i.e., phenomena relating to or involving *quality* or kind. For instance, when we are interested in investigating the reasons for human behaviour (i.e., why people think or do certain things in a certain way), we often talk of 'Motivation Research', an important type of qualitative research. This type of research aims at discovering the underlying motives and desires, using in-depth interviews.

Other techniques of such research are; *word association tests, sentence completion tests, story completion tests* and similar other projective techniques. *Attitude* or *opinion* research; that is research designed to find out how people feel or what they think about a particular subject or institution and also falls under qualitative research. Qualitative research is especially important in the behavioural sciences where the aim is to discover the underlying motives of human behaviour.

Through such research we are able to analyse the various factors which motivate people to behave in a particular manner, or which make people like or dislike a particular thing. It may be stated however, that to apply qualitative research in practice is relatively a difficult job and therefore, while doing such research, one should seek guidance from experts who are very familiar with the use of the method.

d) *Conceptual vs Empirical:* Conceptual research is concerned with abstract idea(s) or theory. It is generally used by philosophers and thinkers to develop new concepts or to reinterpret existing ones. Empirical research focuses strictly on experience or observation, generally ignoring theory as a basis to conduct that research. It is data-based research, coming up with conclusions which are capable of being verified by observation or experiment. Empirical research is also referred to as experimental research. The researcher enters such work armed with facts and a hypothetical proposition.

Such research is thus characterised by the experimenter's control over the variables under study and the researcher's deliberate manipulation of one of them to study its effects. Empirical research is appropriate when proof is sought that certain variables affect other variables in some way. Evidence gathered through experiments or empirical studies is today considered to be the most compelling support for a given hypothesis.

Other Types of Research

All other types of research are variations of one or more of the above stated approaches, based on either the purpose of research or the time required to accomplish research, on the environment in which research is done, or on the basis of some other similar factor. From the point of view of time, we can think of research in terms of:

- *One-time research or longitudinal research*

    In the case of one-time research, the research is strictly one-off engagement while longitudinal research refers to a study over a long period of time, say 20 years. This categorization emphasizes on time and depends on the nature and objective of the study concerned. For example, one would think of a study carried out in a community by the state to establish residents' views just before a major programme as one-time research while a study conducted to find out behavioural changes on long term inmates, say over a period of twenty years, or medical cases of certain patients, fits as longitudinal research.

- *Field-setting research or laboratory research or simulation research*

    This categorization focuses on the environment in which the research is being conducted. For example, field-setting research could be one in which a researcher sets out to investigate communication among primates in the forest; or when a student goes to an IDP camp or a hospital to collect data from participants. Data collected from the field is called field-data and it is usually primary data. A study to test the reaction of a metal on a given chemical can only be conducted in a laboratory. An example of simulation research, on the other hand, is the administration of a trial drug on monkeys to find out the effect the drug might have on humans.

- *Clinical or diagnostic research*

    Clinical research takes small samples and conducts in-depth case studies to draw causal relationships between variables under study. They may use technology to assist in gathering the required data over a period of time. For example, a researcher may pick a small number of individuals suffering from a strange disease and spend one or two years conducting in-depth studies on them to definitively understand the disease, its causes, effects and treatment. Diagnostic research seeks to determine the frequency in which a phenomenon occurs or in which it is associated with something else. For example, a researcher might notice tendency for crime to be prevalent in informal settlements of a city then sets out to find out the frequency, explanation and links between slums and crime.

- *Exploratory or formalized research*

Exploratory research seeks to arrive at hypotheses and not necessarily subject the hypothesis to test while formalized research studies begin with a substantial structure and with specific hypotheses to be tested. An example of an exploratory research could be one in which a researcher sets into a community to understand their general ways of life without any particular cultural position in mind. On the other hand, when a researcher gets to the same community to find out why that community practices burial of the dead, then in that case the research sets out on a formal pre-designed plan with existing hypothetical position.

- *Historical research*

Historical research applies sources that are historical in nature such as archaeological tools etc. to examine events or ideas of the past in order to use such understanding to relate the events to the present. For instance, an archaeologist may want to understand how human communication might have evolved from stone-age to the advent of mobile phones.

- *Conclusion-oriented and decision-oriented research*

Under conclusion-oriented research, a researcher has the latitude (liberty, freedom) to select a problem, design the study and conceptualize the study at will. Decision-oriented research begins with a particular dilemma in mind, usually with no flexibility to select direction of the research. For example, a plant specialist may want to find out climatic conditions under which a particular plant may survive, thus designing a conclusion-oriented research. Similarly, if a government ministry plans to conduct large scale production of rice in its southern part, then it may commission a study to help it make the decision to proceed or abandon the project.

Research Approaches

The above description of the types of research brings to light the fact that there are two basic approaches to research; *quantitative approach* and the *qualitative approach*. The former involves the generation of data in quantitative form which can be subjected to rigorous quantitative analysis in a formal and rigid fashion. This approach can be further sub-classified into *inferential, experimental* and *simulation approaches* to research. The purpose of *inferential approach* to research is to form a data base from which to infer characteristics or relationships of a population. This usually means survey research where a sample of population is studied (questioned or observed) to determine its characteristics, and it is then inferred that the population has the same characteristics.

Experimental approach is characterised by much greater control over the research environment and in this case some variables are manipulated to observe their effect on other variables. *Simulation approach* involves the construction of an artificial environment within which relevant information and data can be generated. This permits observation of the dynamic behaviour of a system (or its sub-system) under controlled conditions. The term 'simulation' in the context of business and social sciences applications refers to "the operation of a numerical model that represents the structure of a dynamic process. Given the values of initial conditions, parameters and exogenous variables, a simulation is run to represent the behaviour of the process over time," (Meir, et. al. 2017). The simulation approach may also be useful in building models for understanding future conditions.

Qualitative approach to research is concerned with subjective (not numerical or statistical) assessment of attitudes, opinions and behaviour.

Research in such a situation is a function of a researcher's insights and impressions of s/he observes. Such an approach to research generates results either in non-quantitative form or in forms which usually are not subjected to rigorous quantitative analysis. Generally, the techniques of focus group discussions (FGD), key informant interviews, face-to-face interviews, projective techniques and in-depth interviews are used to collect data from a specific sample group or participants. All these are explained at length in the chapters that follow.

Significance of Research

The famous Hudson Maxim stated that "all progress is born of inquiry. Doubt is often better than overconfidence, for it leads to inquiry, and inquiry leads to invention," and this is the best context in which the significance of research can well be understood. Increased amounts of research make progress possible. Research inculcates scientific and inductive thinking and promotes the development of logical habits of thinking and organisation. The role of research across the disciplines and professions has greatly increased in modern times. The increasingly complex nature of business and government has focused attention on the use of research in solving operational problems. Research as an aid to economic policy has gained added importance both for government and business.

Research provides the basis for nearly all government policies in our economic system. For instance, government's budgets rest in part on an analysis of the needs and desires of the people and on the availability of revenues to meet these needs. The cost of needs has to be equated to probable revenues and this is a field where research is most needed. Through research we can devise alternative policies and can as well examine and compare the consequences of each of these alternatives. Scholars who consult companies and governments as well as organizations use research to show evidence of their conclusion and suggest remedies to the problems in their recommendations.

Decision-making may not be a part of research, but research certainly facilitates the decisions of the policy maker. Government has also to chalk out programmes for dealing with all facets of the country's existence and most of these will be related directly or indirectly to economic conditions. The plight of cultivators, the problems of small and medium enterprises (SMEs) and large industries, working conditions, trade union activities, the problems of distribution, even the size and nature of defense services are matters requiring research in order for the decision-makers to design a constructive policy, make plausible decisions, and implement them accordingly. Thus, research is considered necessary with regard to the allocation of a nation's resources.

Research has its special significance in solving various operational and planning problems of business and industry. Operations research and market research, along with motivational research, are considered crucial and their results assist in more than one way, in taking business decisions. Market research is the investigation of the structure and development of a market for the purpose of formulating efficient policies for purchasing, production and sales. Operations research refers to the application of mathematical, logical and analytical techniques to the solution of business problems of cost minimization, profit maximization or what can be termed as optimisation problems.

Research is equally important for social scientists in studying social relationships and in seeking answers to various social problems. It likewise provides the intellectual satisfaction of knowing a few things just for the sake of knowledge. Similarly, research also offers a practical utility value to social scientists enabling them do better or more efficiently in serving the society. Research in social sciences is concerned both with knowledge for its own sake and with knowledge for what it can contribute to practical concerns.

In addition to what has been stated above, the significance of research can also be understood keeping in view the following points:

a) To those students who are required to write a Master's or PhD thesis, research may mean a career or a way of attaining a high standing in the social structure;

b) To professionals in research methodology, research may mean a source of livelihood;

c) To philosophers and thinkers, research may mean the outlet for new ideas and insights;

d) To literary men and women, research may mean the development of new styles and creative work;

e) To analysts and intellectuals, research may mean the generalisations of new theories.

Thus, research is the fountain of knowledge for the sake of knowledge and an important source of providing guidelines for solving different business, governmental and social problems.

The Research Process

The research process consists of a series of actions or steps necessary to effectively carry out research and the desired sequencing of these steps. The chart shown in Figure 1.1 illustrates a research process.

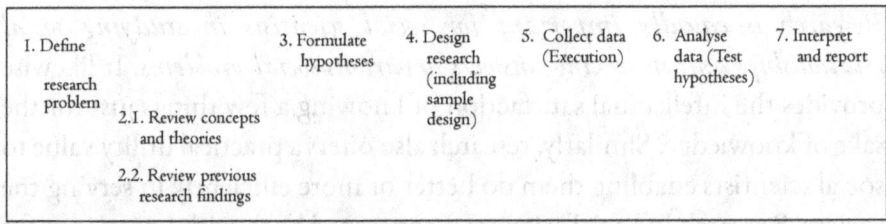

Fig. 1.1: Research process in flow chart

The chart indicates that the research process consists of a number of closely related activities as shown through the flow chart running from 1 to 7. But such activities overlap continuously rather than follow a strictly prescribed sequence. The steps in the chart are related not in a lockstep manner. One step influences other steps that follow. This means that procedures that come later are important and must be taken into account in the early stages. If this is not done, serious challenges may occur that may jeopardise the completion of the study or compromise its quality.

These steps are neither separate or distinct, nor mutually exclusive. Their order is not rigid (inflexible) in the sense of each following the other strictly. The researcher therefore needs to anticipate the requirements of the steps that are subsequent to the one s/he is handling at the time. It is however important to abide by the following order in following the research process:

a) Formulating the research problem;
b) Surveying extensive (related) literature;
c) Developing the hypothesis;
d) Preparing the research design;
e) Determining sample design;
f) Collecting the data;
g) Executing the project;
h) Analysing data;
i) Testing hypothesis;
j) Making generalizations and interpretation;
k) Preparing the report or presenting the results, i.e. formally writing up the conclusions.

Formulating the Research Problem

Research problems occur in two ways. There are research problems that arise due to states of nature and others that occur as a relationship between variables. The researcher, therefore, has the task of determining the research problem from the outset. This involves locating the general area or specific aspect of a subject- matter that is of interest and deserving of research inquiry. The problem should be stated unambiguously but still in a broad general way. The researcher has to consider the feasibility of any solution prior to the formulation of the problem.

The conceptualization and formulation of a research topic from a general topic is the first step in a scientific enquiry. Formulating a research problem involves understanding the research problem clearly and expressing it in meaningful terms from an analytical point of view. The research problem is best understood by discussing it with a researcher's colleagues or with an expert in the specific disciplinary area. In academic institutions, researchers get help from guides or supervisors who are qualified and experienced in research in the discipline area.

Reviewing

With the successful conceptualization and formulation of a research problem, there is need for the researcher to write a synopsis. This is an obligatory requirement for research students pursuing doctoral degrees. They are required to submit the synopsis to a committee or board for approval. After this, it is crucial for a researcher to conduct an extensive review of literature related to the research problem. This may require extensive literature, abstracting and indexing journals, and published or unpublished bibliographies. Other resources that may be useful are academic journals, conference proceedings, government reports and books. In this process, it should be remembered that one source will lead to another. Earlier studies in similar areas or theoretical approaches to the conceptualized problem should also be selected for review. A good library is an invaluable requirement at this stage.

Developing the Hypotheses

The development of working hypotheses in very clear terms follows after the extensive review of literature. A working hypothesis is a tentative assumption made in order to draw out and test its logical or empirical consequences. Working hypotheses afford the whole research process a focal point and significantly affect the manner in which tests are conducted in the analysis of data. They also indirectly affect the quality of data which is required for the analysis. This is why the development of working hypotheses is a very important exercise.

A well-developed working hypothesis should be very specific and limited to the research in which it is developed because it has to be tested. Hypothesis serve as a guide to the researcher in delimiting the area of research and keep the whole research process on track. It sharpens the researcher's thinking, focusing attention on the more significant components of the research problem. In addition, hypothesis points to the type of data required and the type of methods of analysis.

Research Design

With the research problem formulated in clear-cut terms, working hypotheses well-developed, then the researcher prepares a research design. A research design is the conceptual structure within which the study is conducted. The design ensures that the research is as efficient as possible in yielding maximal information within the limits of the research objective. It also provides for the collection of relevant evidence by minimizing expenditure of effort, time and money.

The development of a good research design depends significantly on the purpose of the research. Research purposes come in four categories as follows:

a) Exploration,
b) Description,
c) Diagnosis, and
d) Experimentation.

Exploratory research seeks to gain familiarity with a phenomenon or to achieve new insights into it. For example, a geologist may want to understand the general profile of a location and its potential. To do so, an exploratory research suffices.

Descriptive research seeks to accurately portray the characteristics of a particular individual, situation or group. For example, a researcher seeking to understand and fully describe the political organization of Somalia may want to employ descriptive design in order to capture all the details of the polity's organization.

Diagnostic research seeks to determine the frequency with which a phenomenon occurs or with which it is associated with something else. For example, a researcher may want to establish the links between informal settlements and the tendency to engage in crime using a diagnostic approach.

Experimental approach is characterized by setting a specified research environment to manipulate some variables with a view to observe their effect on other variables. For example, an agriculturalist may want to expose some crops to sun while denying the others in order to find out the effect of the presence or absence of the sun to the crops.

A flexible research design provides an opportunity for considering many different aspects of a problem if its purpose is exploration. However, if the purpose is an accurate description of a situation or a relationship between variables, the appropriate design has to minimize bias and maximize the reliability of the data collected and analysed.

Sampling

All the items or persons that form the entire target of a study are referred to as a 'population'. However, studying of an entire population is usually nearly impossible; as such a researcher has to make a careful decision on the size of the research population that will be representative of the population. This decision is termed as *sampling*, which is achieved by formulating a *sample design*. For example, a plan to select 12 of a city's 200 drugstores for a study is a sample design. A sample can be a probability sample or a non-probability sample. Probability samples are samples that are randomly selected, according to the entire population with an equal chance of selection while non-probability samples are based on some subjective judgment of the researcher depending on the purpose of the research. In the case of probability samples, a researcher may be interested in a population of government ministers in a study, thus could design a sample that selects the recommended number of the ministers but which allows any minister an equal opportunity to be selected to participate in the research. Conversely, a researcher may be targeting religious women with more than five children in a multi-religious, liberal neighbourhood where more religious women are the minority. In this case, a non-probabilistic sample suffices.

Data Collection

At any time that a study is investigating a real-life problem, the data at hand is inadequate. But it is very necessary to collect data that is appropriate. Several ways are available for collecting the appropriate data, but which differ in the context of costs in terms of money, time and other resources that the researcher can mobilise. A researcher may collect primary data either through conducting an experiment or running a survey. In the case of an experiment, the researcher will conduct an experiment and observe quantitative measurements, or the data, which s/he will use to examine the truth in his hypothesis.

Project Execution

This is a critical component of the research process. If this stage proceeds well and the project is executed in a systematic manner and in time, the data collected should be adequate and dependable. If the survey employs structured questionnaires, and the data is machine-processed, then the questions and the possible answers may be coded. However, if the data is collected through interviewers, there is need for arrangements to be made for the interviewers to be properly selected and trained. Such training should be aided by the use of instruction manuals that explain the tasks of the interviewers in clear detail at each step. After data collection, the researcher will embark on data analysis.

Data Analysis

Data analysis requires the establishment and application of categories to raw data through coding, tabulation and then drawing statistical inferences. In this process, unwieldy (bulky, heavy) data is best condensed into a few manageable groups and tables for further analysis. It is therefore essential for the researcher to classify raw data into purposeful and usable categories. *Coding*, an operation that involves categories of data being transformed into symbols that may be tabulated and counted is done at this stage.

However, coding requires another *editing* which is the procedure that improves the quality of the data. After coding, the researcher moves to the tabulation stage at which the classified data is put in the form of tables, the mechanical devices used at this juncture. Data, especially in large inquiries, is tabulated by computers, not only to save time but also to enable a study to compare large numbers of variables affecting a problem simultaneously.

Criteria for Good Research

All types of research work and studies must meet the common ground of a scientific method that they all employ. Scientific research must therefore satisfy the following criteria:

a) The purpose of the research and common concepts to be used should be clearly defined.

b) The study must describe the research procedure it uses in enough detail to enable another researcher to replicate the study for further advancement and the continuity of what has already been achieved.

c) The researcher must plan the procedural design of the study carefully in order to yield results that are as objective as possible.

d) The study should be reported frankly and weaknesses in the procedural design should also be reported, and their effects estimated upon the findings.

e) The data analysis should be conducted adequately in order to reveal its significance. The methods of analysis used should be appropriate and the validity and reliability of the data should be ensured.

f) Conclusions, when drawn, should be restricted only to those justified by the data of the research and limited only to those for which the data provided an adequate basis.

g) A study warrants greater confidence only if the researcher has adequate experience, a good reputation in research, and is a person of integrity.

Other qualities of a good research include the fact that good research is systematic. Good research must have a structure that has specific steps to be taken in a predictable and specific order that meets a well-defined set of rules. The fact that research needs to be systematic does not in any case dismiss creativity as a requirement of research. It however rules out guesswork and intuition in arriving at conclusions. Good research is also logic. This means that research proceeds by the rules of logical reasoning as borne out in processes of induction and deduction. The process of induction means reasoning from a part to the whole whereas deduction involves reasoning from a premise to a conclusion which follows from that very premise. This requirement makes research more meaningful in the context of decision making.

One other equally important quality of good research is the fact that good research is empirical. This requirement means that research relates to the aspects of a real situation and deals with concrete data that forms a basis for meeting the external validity to research results. Good research is also replicable. Research results should stand the test of proof by providing opportunities for verification by a replication of the study and thereby building a sound basis for making decisions.

Limitation of Research Methods

The Weaknesses of Quantitative Research Methodology

The strengths of quantitative research can also be its weaknesses. Many important characteristics of people and communities including both rich and poor for example, their identities, perceptions, and beliefs cannot be meaningfully reduced to numbers or adequately understood without reference to the local context in which people live (Dudwick et al, 2006).

Effective quantitative research usually requires a large sample size, sometimes several thousand households. However, lack of resources sometimes makes large-scale research of this kind impossible. In many settings, particularly in developing countries, interested parties (e.g. governments, Non-Governmental Organizations and public service providers) may lack the skills and especially the resources needed to conduct a thorough quantitative evaluation (Dudwick et al, 2006).

In terms of disaster survey, the shortcoming of quantitative data is that it fails to provide an in-depth description of the experience of the people affected by the disaster. Knowing how many people are affected and their locations does not provide sufficient information to guide agencies and service providing sectors on what they should plan for in terms of response (ACAPS, 2012).

The Weaknesses of Qualitative Research Methodology

There are three major drawbacks associated with qualitative cultural analysis. First, the process is time-consuming. Second, a potential problem of a particular issue can go unnoticed. Third, the researchers' interpretations may be limited because of the position of the subjects, personal experience and knowledge which influence the observations and conclusions. In addition, since qualitative inquiry is generally open-ended, the participants have more control over the content of the data collected (Yauch and Steudel, 2003).

Further to the three aforementioned drawbacks, there are also limitations of qualitative research associated with the data. A research manual by ACAPS outlines three such weaknesses inherent in qualitative data. First, data results are not generally objectively verifiable. Second, it requires a labour-intensive analysis process such as categorization, and recoding, among other things. Third, it needs skilled interviewers to successfully carry out the primary data collection activities (ACAPS, 2012).

It is imperative to also note that advancements in technology have also pervaded research, a practice presenting both boon and bane to qualitative and quantitative methods. More pre-eminently in the 21st Century, researchers have employed sophisticated automated machines such as Unmanned Aerial Vehicles (aka UAVs or drones) to carry out research. This technology has increasingly been employed in geographical surveys, archeological mapping, determining populations in congested areas, and wildlife census, among many others. Such technology tends to favour quantitative research, easing surveys and providing preliminary descriptive data. However, due to the inability of these machines to foster human interactions with subjects of research, they are usually insufficient in the case of research which is ideally qualitative in nature. Researchers thus need to take necessary caution not to over-employ technology, as the human component of research still remains a fundamental tenet even in the age of technology.

End of Chapter 1 Quiz

a) Think of a phenomenon which might require a researcher to seek familiarity (with the phenomenon) and frequency of the phenomenon. Describe the phenomenon in a paragraph.

b) Citing examples, distinguish between types and approaches to research.

c) A researcher observes that members of a given community have the tendency to protect their own when interacting with others outside their community. The most appropriate approach to finding out the explanation for this behaviour would be (quantitative, qualitative) research.

d) Explain your answer for (c) above.

e) In two paragraphs of 5-6 sentences each, write a problem statement for question (a) above.

SOCIAL SCIENCE AND RESEARCH METHODS: THE HISTORY

> *"Although instances of scientific progress have been documented over many centuries, the terms "science," "scientists," and the "scientific method" were coined only in the 19th century."*
>
> — Anol Bhattacherjee (2012)

Introduction

This section provides a historical overview of social science research methods and methodology over the years. The section begins with a brief introduction of the development of social science as an academic discipline. This is then followed by the main discourse that traces the historical development of research methods and methodology in social sciences. The section then concludes with a brief suggestion on the way forward for social science research methods and the future of social sciences as a scientific academic discipline.

The Development of Social Sciences as a Scientific Discipline: An Overview

To understand the historical development of social science research methods, it is important to first comprehend what science in general is and what social science is in particular. Science can be described as a systematic and organized body of knowledge in any field of inquiry using a scientific method (Bhattacherjee, 2012). There are two main branches of science; *natural science* and *social science.*

While natural sciences involve the study of naturally occurring phenomenon and events, social sciences mainly involve the study of people or groups of people and how they behave either as individuals or within group settings (Bhattacherjee, 2012). These two major branches of science are further sub- divided into various branches depending on the academic disciplines of study. For instance, natural sciences may involve the study of biological, physical or earth sciences, while social science may involve the study of sociology, economics, and political science amongst other disciplines. However, in this section, the main area of focus will be the evolution of social sciences with a specific focus on the historical evolution of social science research methodologies.

Although sociological sciences such as political science, history, and anthropology are relatively new areas of academic disciplines as compared to natural sciences, the logic behind their rise as academic and scientific fields of study can be traced to the blends of general human knowledge and psychology. Nevertheless, the refined development of sociological sciences started to take shape in the 19th Century (Ritchie and Lewis, 2003). This drive was mainly pushed by the rise of modernity and the need to provide explanations for social integration and disintegration among human beings, which had been witnessed in the mid to late 18th century and published by thinkers such as Hobbes's "Leviathan," Lock's "Two Treaties of Government," and Montesquieu's "Spirit of Laws (Ibid.).

Following along these trends, Augustus Comte in 1838 coined the term *sociology* from Latin word *Socious*, meaning "companion", and *logos* a Greek word meaning "associate". However, unlike modern scientific studies, divided into either natural or sociological sciences, Comte's understanding of sociology embraced all forms of science (Bhattacherjee, 2012). These developments led to the establishment of the first department dedicated to the study of sociology in 1892 at the University of Chicago. The study of sociology has since then continued to be divided into various specific academic disciplines.

Historical Transformation of Social Science Research Methodology

In order to understand the evolution of science research methods, it is first important to define what social science research methodology is all about. Kothari defines research methods as all the methods and techniques that are used to conduct research (Kothari, 2004). Kothari goes further to differentiate between research method and methodology by stating that unlike research methods, methodology is the systematic approach to solving a research problem, including the various steps and logic behind solving the problem (Ibid.).

The earliest indications of social science research were commissioned by governments to determine populations within territories for the purpose of taxation, drafting citizens into armies, or for general planning (Crothers and Platt, 2003). Amongst the earliest recorded census were by the Chinese dynasties dating back to almost 400 years ago. The other earliest civilisations known to have undertaken census included ancient Egyptians, Persians, Romans, and Greeks (Ibid.). For instance, the five yearly censuses undertaken by the Romans were much more detailed forms of social science research as they required data collection of all adult males which were later stored for possible use in the future (Ibid.).

In Europe, during the medieval times, evidence of engagement in research was witnessed upon the discovery of the *Domesday Book* of 1086, which determined landholding in the 11th century England following the orders of King William I.

These early research efforts could not be tested for important standards that determine the quality of research today like objectivity. However, evidence of objectivity in research emerged in the 17th century in the wake of Descartes' publication of *"Discourse on Methodology"* (Ritchie and Lewis, 2003). He mainly singled out the need for evidence in explaining causes of events and phenomena while avoiding subjectivity in analysis. Following in the footsteps of Descartes, Francis Bacon and Isaac Newton in their writings acknowledged the need for making assumptions on the basis of empirical rather than theoretical approach (Ibid.). David Hume, greatly acknowledged as the pioneer of the empirical research method, later supported this approach by stating that knowledge was generated by human experiences in accordance with the senses.

The development of these schools of thought was later backed by Auguste Comte's explanations that just like the natural sciences, sociology could be studied by invoking the invariant laws (Blanchard, 1918). These explanations would later give rise to the development of positivism theory that dominated much of the 20th century social science research methods. The six fundamental principles of positivism include:

a) Social science can be studied in the same way as natural sciences,
b) Only observable phenomena are seen as knowledge,
c) Inductive acquisition of knowledge,
d) Deductive derivation of hypotheses,
e) Observations reconcile theoretical misunderstandings,
f) Facts and values are distinct (Denzin and Lincoln, 1998).

However, following the publication of *"Critique of Pure Reason"* by Emmanuel Kant in 1781, a new paradigm in social science research methods emerged to counter positivism. This new school of thought came to beknown as the interpretivist theory. Kant's four main arguments that led to this new understanding were primed on these facts: senses are used to interpret perceptions, knowledge could be derived from thinking not just experiences, knowledge was beyond mere empirical enquiry, and there exists a difference between "scientific" and "practical" reasoning (Ritchie and Lewis, 2003). These principles postulated by Kant which gave way to the interpretivist theory, formed the basis of qualitative research methods which have tremendously gained ground on the research study of social sciences.

With the development of the interpretivist theory, more reasons emerged to counter its meaningfulness as a means of conducting social science research. The post-structuralism and deconstructionists, led by Denzel and Lincoln, started to question qualitative research method's explanations of objectivity, time and meanings. According to them, the social scientists could not develop a fixed definition of terms because definitions were dynamic and changed according to different locations and times in history. Any attempt to have a fixed set of definitions in social sciences would therefore lead to bias as it suppressed diversity (Denzin and Lincoln, 1998).

As social science developed into the twentieth century, more approaches emerged in social science research methods challenging the previous approaches. Some of these approaches include *Marxism, neo-Marxism* as well as *Feminism*. Their main underlying argument was that there was need to inculcate gender, politics, race and other social identities into the study of social sciences since they greatly influenced human life (Porta and Keating, 2008).

Nevertheless, way into the 21st Century, the debate has continued to be broadly defined between advocates of qualitative versus quantitative research methods in the study of social sciences. However, based on the comparative advantage and disadvantage of positivism versus interpretivism, most scholars have started to embrace cross-fertilization of these two paradigms in social science research methods and methodology. Triangulations can be used to incorporate different research methods and methodologies across social sciences; however, it is much more difficult to triangulate specific research epistemologies due to their competing schools of thought (Porta and Keating, 2008).

Conclusions

With the advances in information technology, social science research methods and methodology are expected to increasingly be more efficient in data collection and data analysis methods compared to the past decades. There is also a need for the various disciplines and sub-disciplines to develop social science research methods and methodology that are specific to their own niche of study to avoid the tiring debates on which research methods are more appropriate in the general study of social sciences.

End of Chapter 2 Quiz

a) Briefly explain the fundamental justifications for terming the study of social phenomena as science.

b) Human interactions is to a social scientist what a laboratory is to a natural scientist. Exhaustively discuss this statement in groups.

c) As in (b) above, the philosophical foundation of research methods is the fact that it aims to enquire. True or false?

CHAPTER 03
EPISTEMOLOGICAL ASPECTS OF RESEARCH

"Epistemology matters. It is not just fascinating in itself; its concerns arise in every serious form of human inquiry."

— Timothy Williamson (2014)

Introduction

As part of the debate over the epistemological aspects of research, Hallebone and Priest (2009) define epistemology as a branch of philosophy that deals with the sources of knowledge. It is also concerned with possibilities, nature, sources and limitations of knowledge in the field of study (Hallebone and Priest, 2009). Knowledge comprises the acquisition of information, awareness and understanding of particular aspects of reality. It is the clear, lucid information gained through the process of reason applied to reality. Tennis (2008) explains that it is the claim on what knowledge is valid in research on the organization of knowledge, and therefore what constitutes acceptable sources of evidence and acceptable end results of knowledge (Tennis, 2008). Epistemology has to do with the creation and dissemination of knowledge in particular areas of inquiry.

According to Becker (1970), epistemology has characteristically concerned itself with what ought to be rather than what it is. Epistemology therefore settles its questions by reasoning from first principles rather than by empirical investigation. Crotty (2003) argues that epistemology is concerned with providing a philosophical grounding for deciding what kinds of knowledge are possible and how we can ensure that they are both adequate and legitimate (Crotty, 2003). It raises questions like "What is knowledge? How is knowledge acquired? What do people know? What are the necessary and sufficient conditions of knowledge? What is its structure, and what are its limits? What makes justified beliefs justified? How are we to understand the concept of justification? Is justification internal or external to one's own mind?"

In research, there are numerous sources of knowledge. First, there is *intuitive knowledge* which differs from all forms of mediated knowledge as it generally involves conceptualizing the object of knowledge by means of rational or analytical thought processes. Intuition is the ability to acquire knowledge without inference or the use of reason. It is based on intuition, faith and beliefs. Human feelings play a greater role in intuitive knowledge compared to reliance on facts (Crotty, 2003). This type of knowledge can be used in order to select a specific problem to be explored within a selected research area.

Second is *authoritarian knowledge*. This type of knowledge relies on information that has been acquired through information available from book sources, research papers, experts' opinions and supreme powers. It is gained during the process of literature review. The third type is *logical knowledge* which is a creation of new knowledge through the application of logical reasoning. Logical knowledge is generated as a result of analysing primary data. The last type of knowledge is *empirical knowledge*. It is defined as a type of knowledge that relies on objective facts that have been established and can be demonstrated. After primary data has been collected, the findings and conclusions of the research can be perceived as empirical knowledge.

Epistemology has two key components: *interpretivism* and *positivism*.

Interpretivism

Interpretivism is a term used to identify approaches to social science that share particular ontological and epistemological assumptions. It assumes that people create and associate their own subjective and inter-subjective meanings as they interact with the world around them (Orlikowski, 1991).

Interpretivist research entails interpretation of the elements of the study as it integrates human interest into a study. Accordingly, interpretive researchers assume that access to reality is only through social constructions such as language, consciousness, shared meanings and instruments (Collins, 2010).

According to the interpretivist approach, it is important for the researcher -- as a social actor -- to appreciate differences between people. There are several levels of interpretation- for example, the interpretation of the meaning of what has been said and this is from the observer's interpretation of what the originator of the text meant to communicate but limited by the observer's interpretation of the originator's life world bounded by the originator's own life world (Collins, 2010). Additionally, reality is socially constructed. The goal of research is to understand and not to predict phenomena. Its focus of interest is what is specific, unique, and deviant (Mansfield, 1992).

Additionally, by positing that a reality cannot be divorced or removed from our knowledge, the interpretivist paradigm claims that the values of researchers exist in all phases of the research process. In this paradigm, truth is understood to be negotiated and determined through dialogue. Findings or knowledge claims are therefore created during the process of investigation and therefore emerge through a process of dialogue during which conflicting and varying interpretations are negotiated among members of a community. Thus, in the evaluation of interpretive science, pragmatic and moral concerns are key considerations. Fostering a dialogue between researchers and respondents is critical (Blumer, 1984). It is through this dialectical process that a more informed and sophisticated understanding of the social world can be created. Moreover, all interpretations are based on a particular moment. That is, they are located in a particular context or situation and time. They are open to re- interpretation and negotiation through conversation (Angen, 2000).

The interpretivist approach is based on a naturalistic approach of data collection such as interviews and observations. Secondary data research is also popular with the interpretivist philosophy. In this type of studies, meanings emerge usually towards the end of the research process. Interpretivist approach is based on **relativist ontology** and **transactional or subjectivist epistemology.** Relativist ontology perceives reality as inter-subjective that is based on meanings and understandings on social and experiential levels. According to **transactional or subjectivist epistemology**, people cannot be separated from their knowledge; therefore, there is a clear link between the researcher and research subject (Nilson, 1992).

Interpretivist positions are founded on the theoretical belief that reality is socially constructed and fluid. Thus, what we know is always negotiated within cultures, social settings and relationships with other people. From this perspective, validity or truth cannot be grounded in an objective reality; what is taken to be valid or true is negotiated and there can be multiple, valid claims to knowledge.

Angen (2000) offers the following criteria for evaluating research from an interpretivist perspective: *First,* one needs to give careful consideration and articulation of the research question. *Second,* inquiries should be carried out in a respectful manner and the researchers should be aware of and articulate, in the choices and interpretations they make during the inquiry process, evidence of taking responsibility for those choices. *Third,* validity becomes a moral question for Angen (2000) and must be located in the discourse of the research community.

There are two types of validity: *ethical* validity and *substantive* validity. Ethical validity refers to the recognition that the choices we make through the research process have political and ethical considerations. Substantive validity refers to evaluating the substance or content of an interpretive work and the need to see in the evidence of the interpretive choices the researcher made, an assessment of the biases inherent in the work over the lifespan of a research project and that the research should self-reflect to understand our own transformation in the research process (Angen, 2000).

In conclusion, primary data generated in interpretivist studies cannot be generalized since data is heavily impacted by personal viewpoints and values. Therefore, to a certain extent, reliability and representativeness of data is undermined, although certain scholars disagree with this notion. The enquiry should explore how knowledge is produced and who is mandated to produce it, how it circulates, how some knowledge is taken to be authoritative while the other knowledge is marginalized, and how some forms of knowledge are taken to be credible by certain categories of actors or contested by others.

Positivism

Positivism was developed in the 1990s, by a group of Austrian intellectuals, mostly scientists and mathematicians, although it traces its roots to the works of French philosopher Auguste Comte in the 1800s. This school of thought analyses descriptive tools and concepts of science in a bid to describe reality. Positivism is therefore a meta-descriptive account of reality. Positivism is in accordance with the empiricist view that knowledge stems from human experience and that all factual knowledge is based on experience (Holier, 2011).

Positivists contend that theology, metaphysics and the positive schools of thought are involved in the process of understanding the idea of reality. Theology, also known as mythology, holds to the presence of a supernatural being responsible for the creation of the world and what is in it as the determinant of what is real. This definition was discredited as loaded with political implications thereby creating the need for the development of another approach to reality.

Hume believed that it was not possible to conceive knowledge outside of what is observable. A knowledge claim is therefore simply the associations made on the basis of observations. Positivist research methods come in the form of those methods that can be controlled, measured and used to support a hypothesis. It can be concluded that positivism as an epistemological approach explains causal relationships using scientific methods based on logic and mathematics. In this case therefore, scientific methods are the source of all authoritative knowledge and that the researcher and the object of research are two independent ideas (Holier, 2011). Positivism can therefore be defined as a philosophy of science which asserts that positive facts or information is derived from sensory experiences and is interpreted through rational, logical and mathematical treatments. These processes thus are the source of all authoritative knowledge (Macionis and Linda, 2010).

Assumptions of Positivism

The theory of positivism has numerous assumptions which include:

First, in prediction and control, there are general patterns of cause and effect that can be used to predict and control natural phenomena. As a result, general patterns of cause and effect are used to predict and control natural phenomena.

Second, in empirical verification, one cannot rely on one's own perceptions of the world. This means that for data to be accurate, there has to be strict methodological protocol. The role of the researcher is limited to data collection and interpretation through an objective approach. Consequently, in order to avoid the problem of subjective biases, the experiences and values of human beings should not be included in research.

Third, the tenet of neutralism suggests that the principles of natural sciences ought to be applicable to social sciences. In this case therefore, the methodology that is used in natural sciences can also be applied to human beings and the society.

The fourth tenet is the concept of phenomenalism. This means that observable phenomena provide valid information; that which cannot be observed is not necessary and does not constitute evidence in the practice of research. Research findings are quantifiable and observable; it depends on quantifiable observations that in turn lead themselves to statistical analysis.

The fifth assumption is the idea of atomism where things can be studied by reducing them to their smallest parts to get the best results. In this case, mental phenomena may be able to be reduced to behavioural phenomena then reduced to biology then to physics. Everything can therefore be studied as physical phenomena by movements in space and time (Kincaid, 1998).

Lastly, positivism posits that scientific laws should be used in the study of research. The society, like the physical world, operates according to certain general laws. The goal of science is therefore to create generalized laws that are useful for prediction both in natural and social sciences (Ibid.).

Application in Research

Positivism relies more on quantitative methods of research i.e., experimental and manipulative methods. Quantitative methods are systematic empirical investigations of observable phenomenon via statistical, mathematical and computable techniques. It seeks to develop and employ mathematical model theories or hypotheses pertaining to phenomena (Given, 2008). Quantitative methods in this case ensure that there is a distinction between subjective biases and the objective reality studied. This method involves hypothesis generation and testing (Kincaid, 1998). Quantitative methods include methods of data collection and analysis which includes; correlation analysis, regression analysis, mean, mode and median amongst others (Denscombe, 2004).

In this case, research is evaluated based on three criteria; i.e., *validity, reliability* and *generalizability*. Validity refers to the extent to which a measurement or procedure gives the correct answer. It encompasses the experimental concept and establishes whether the results obtained meet all the requirements of scientific research methods. This will allow the researcher to evaluate an objective reality. There are two types of validity; *internal validity* which dictates how the design of an experiment is structured. It encompasses all steps of scientific research, and *external validity* which is the process of examining whether there are other possible causal relationships (Shuttleworth, 2008).

Reliability is the tendency of measurement approaches or procedures to provide the same answer whenever they are carried out. In this case, any significant results must be sustained and more than a one-off finding, and should have an inherent capacity for repeatability. When performed under the same condition by different researchers, an experiment should be able to generate the same results. This will reinforce the findings and ensure acceptability of the hypothesis within the scientific community. When results cannot be replicated, then the experiment will fail the requirements of testability (Shuttleworth, 2008).

Generalizability refers to the extent to which the findings of a study can be applied outside the study context. It involves drawing broad conclusions from particular observations. It is applicable in quantitative sciences but is controversial in qualitative research, which rather seeks to provide a rich, contextualized understanding of some aspects of human experiences through rigorous study of some cases (Denise and Cheryl, 2010).

Post-positivism

Post-positivist research principles emphasize meaning and the creation of new knowledge and are able to support committed social movements, that is, movements that aspire to change the world and contribute towards social justice (Anne, 2006). Post-positivism provides the researcher with more subjective measures for gathering information. The degree of honesty of the researcher could be a problem in this kind of research. Their values in research are not about being neither subjective nor objective, and nor do they prefer subjectivity over objectivity. They believe that multiplicity and complexity are hallmarks of humanity. Post-positivist approaches are interpretive and has led to an emphasis on meaning, seeing the person, experience and knowledge as multiple, relational and not bounded by reason (Henriques et. al.,1998).

Post-positivism has also reawakened questions about the uses and purposes of research, research practice and research knowledge, which are at least as much ethical as they are technical. The post-positivist stance asserts the value of values, passion and politics in research. Research in this mode requires an ability to see the whole picture, to take a distanced view or an overview. The emphasis is on good principles, adequate for working with human participants in all their complexity. Procedures, techniques and methods, while important, must always be subject to ethical scrutiny (Anne, 2006).

Post-positivists posit that research is broad rather than specialised; in this case, a lot of different things qualify as research. Theory and practice cannot be kept separate. We cannot afford to ignore theory just for the sake of facts.

The researcher's motivations for and commitment to research are central and crucial to the enterprise. Post-positivists strive to disrupt the predictability that can occur in traditional interviews. Post-positivist researchers do not see themselves as inevitably solving the problems they set out to investigate. Research can answer questions and indicate causes but equally, research can be about problem setting i.e., coming up with the right questions (Schartz and Walker, 1995).

Conclusions

In conclusion, positivism works well within natural but not social sciences; it has both negative and positive sides to it. First, it is almost impossible to detach one from research activities as an expression is a product of the instincts. Most of the time, the researchers' experiences play a big role in influencing the research results. Therefore, positivism fails to take into account the human ability to interpret experiences and express them to others (Cohen et. al., 2007).

Secondly, inaccurate scientific data alters end results of hypotheses. Experiments could be faulty as most of them are affected by different factors within the environment. Moreover, in a field study, if participants choose random answers, the responses might end up being incorrect yet the researcher has to abide by the findings since there is no flexibility as is with other methods of research (Johnson and Omwegbuzie, 2014).

End of Chapter 3 Quiz

a) As a researcher, critically discuss the limitations of intuition as a source of knowledge.

b) Think of two different research phenomena to which you can apply either interpretivism or positivism and discuss each of the scenarios, demonstrating their application in real life situations.

c) What are the differences between the two schools of thought?

INTRODUCTION TO QUANTITATIVE RESEARCH

"Quantitative research is about explaining phenomena by collecting quantitative data which are analyzed using mathematically-based methods."

— **Suphat Sukamolsom (2007)**

Introduction

This section provides an overview to the introduction of quantitative research methods. It begins by defining quantitative research and the key elements that define quantitative research methods. It also covers the foundations of quantitative research and most appropriate time to use quantitative research methods. This is then followed by the type of quantitative research methods and the process in designing non experiential methods. The section then concludes with a brief suggestion on the way forward for quantitative research methods and the future of quantitative research methods.

What is Quantitative Research?

Aliaga and Gunderson (2000) describe quantitative research methods as a tool for 'explaining phenomena by collecting numerical data that are analyzed using mathematically based methods (in particular statistics)'. The first element in this definition is *explaining "phenomena"*. This is a key element of all research. Therefore, when we conduct research, we are always looking to explain something like why students fail the research methods course. The next critical element that defines quantitative research is the *collection of numerical data.* This is closely connected to the final part of the definition: an *analysis using mathematically based methods.* In order to be able to use mathematically based methods, our data have to be in numerical form. Therefore, quantitative research is essentially about collecting numerical data to explain a particular phenomenon. The last part of the definition refers to the use of mathematically based methods, in particular statistics, to analyse the data (Muijs, 2004).

Quantitative approach involves collecting and converting data into numerical form so that statistical calculations can be made and conclusions drawn. It includes designs, techniques and measures that produce discrete numerical or quantifiable data, as in experimental research, causal-comparative research and co-relational research. It sometimes yields qualitative data depending on the kind of questions asked. For example, descriptive surveys are typically quantitative but the use of open-ended questions gives respondents an opportunity to express their views in a way that provides qualitative data. This approach is based on the positivist philosophical paradigm which holds that one reality exists and that researchers can discover this reality within some realms of probability. This paradigm assumes that there is a discrete distance maintained between the researcher and the object of study, and there should be no influence on it because such influence would produce biased results (Johnson and Christensen, 2011).

Quantitative research uses the deductive or confirmatory or "top down" scientific method. It is used primarily for description, explanation and prediction. It is based on quantitative data, and in particular, on the analysis of variables. The results are statistical and the goal is to generalize the results (Johnson and Christensen, 2011). Creswell (2007), describes it as one in which the investigator primarily uses post positivist claims for developing knowledge (i.e., cause and effect thinking, reduction to specific variables, hypotheses and questions, use of measurement and observation and the test of theories). It employs strategies of inquiry such as experiments and surveys, and collects data using predetermined instruments or responses that yield statistical data.

Foundations of Quantitative Research Methods

The difference between quantitative and qualitative research is often seen as quite fundamental. Many researchers define their methods as either quantitative or qualitative. This idea is linked to what is seen as the different underlying philosophies and world views of researchers in the two 'paradigms' (also called 'epistemologies'). According to this view, two fundamentally different world views underlie quantitative and qualitative research. The quantitative view is described as being 'realist' or sometimes 'positivist', while the world view underlying qualitative research is viewed as being 'subjectivist'. Realists take the view that what research does is to uncover an existing reality. The truth is out there and it is the job of the researcher to use objective research methods to uncover that truth. This means that the researcher needs to be as detached from the research as much as possible, and use methods that maximize objectivity and minimize the involvement of the researcher in the research. This is best done by methods taken largely from the natural sciences which are then transposed to social research settings (Hallebone and Priest, 2009).

When Do We Use Quantitative Methods?

The main question that we need to ask ourselves is 'what kind of questions are best answered by using quantitative as opposed to qualitative methods?' There are four main types of research questions that quantitative research is particularly suited to finding an answer to:

1) Demanding a quantitative answer. For example: How many research method course teachers do we need and how many do we have in our university?

2) Numerical change questions. For example: Are the numbers of post graduate students in our university rising or falling?

3) Finding out the state of something or explaining phenomena. For example: What factors predict the retention of research method course teachers at the university? What factors are related to changes

in student achievement over time? These kinds of questions can be studied successfully by quantitative methods. Many statistical techniques have been developed that allow us to predict scores on one factor, or variable (e.g. teacher retention) from scores on one or more other factors, or variables (e.g. unemployment rates, pay, conditions etc.).

4) Testing of hypotheses. For example: Whether there is a relationship between post graduate students' attitudes toward the research course and the teachers' skills in research methods. Using quantitative research, we can try to test this kind of model.

Please NOTE that quantitative social research is usually organised around the aim of testing theory. A common practice in quantitative social research is to review both theoretical and research literature with the aim of summarizing previous research in the form of a causal model. This model of the contingent relationships between theoretical concepts is then translated into a model of variables or indicators of concepts that informs a research design. The data analysis is then conducted to evaluate the relative importance of each causal variable in the model or to determine whether the most important causal mechanisms are operating to determine outcomes (Blalock, 1989).

Types of Quantitative Research

According to Muijs (2004), there are two main types of quantitative research design:

1) *Experimental designs.* These are sometimes known as 'the scientific method' due to their popularity in scientific research from where they originated. The basis of the experimental method is the experiment, which can be defined as: *a test under controlled conditions that is made to demonstrate a known truth or examine the validity of a hypothesis.* When doing an experiment, we want to control the environment as much as possible and only concentrate on those variables that we want to study.

2) *Non-experimental designs.* In contrast to experimental research, which is a clearly defined research method, non-experimental quantitative research is more varied. Non-experimental methods include survey research, historical research, observation and analysis of existing data sets.

Designing Non-experimental Studies (Survey)

The most common methods in social science research include: *survey research, observational research* and *analysing existing data sets.* Survey research is the most popular (quantitative) research design in the social sciences. Survey research designs are quite flexible and can therefore appear in a variety of forms, but all are characterised by the collection of data using standard questionnaire forms administered by telephone or face-to-face, by postal pencil-and-paper questionnaires or increasingly by using web-based and e-mail forms (Balnaves and Caputi, 2001).

The phases in designing a survey study are similar to any other research. The differences lie in how the study, instruments and data collection are designed. The following are the phases in designing a survey study:

Steps	Summary
Define Research Objectives	Any research design starts with formulating the research objectives. Your research objectives describe what you want to study and how. You need to spell out clearly what the aims of your research are. Research objectives need to be Simple, Measurable, Achievable, Realistic and Time bound (SMART). Also, you must understand that you cannot do everything.

Steps	Summary
2. Formulate Hypotheses	Make predictions about relationships between variables in the form of hypotheses (e.g., 'there is a relationship between student's attitudes and teachers' skills in research methods). However, not all survey studies test specific hypotheses. Whether one wants to test specific hypotheses or conduct a more descriptive study will depend on one's research question or research objective.
3. Define the Population and Sample	The population is the group you want to generalize your findings to. We will then usually want to generalize the results we find in our sample to our population. In order for us to be able to generalize, we need to have an unbiased sample of the population, which means that we want our sample to be representative of the population we are studying. The best way of ensuring that our sample is unbiased is by using probability sampling methods. NOTE: *Sampling method will be discussed in Chapter 7 on Research Design and Management.*
4. Design Research Instruments	In the quantitative approach, the tools used are systematic and pre-defined before the research commences. Data collection instruments include a written questionnaire, a phone questionnaire or an online survey questionnaire. Designing an instrument is a very important process because once the data is collected, we will not be able to rectify any problems with the instruments. It is clear that the quality of the data will depend on the quality of the instruments.

Steps	Summary
5. Collect the Data	In the quantitative approach, the research takes place in an environment in which the researcher is not part of. The data is independent of people's perceptions and, as a result is said to be objective. Quantitative data is depicted as hard, reliable data and is collected based on precise measurement. They use structured and validated data collection instruments. Both qualitative and quantitative methods use interviews, observations, written documents and questionnaires. In this approach, the questionnaire is also closed while in the qualitative approach, the questionnaire is open. Data can be collected through pencil-and-paper questionnaires, telephone or face-to-face interviews and online methods such as web-based questionnaire. NOTE: *Different types of data collection methods will be discussed in Chapter 8 on Data Collection Methods.*
6. Analyse the Data	The final step is data analysis. We can use a large variety of methods when analyzing survey data. These include descriptive (central measure of tendencies, dispersions, tabulations etc.) and inferential statistics (correlations, regression analysis etc.) NOTE: *These will be discussed in Chapter 9 on Data Analysis and Interpretation.*

Conclusions

The quantitative research method allows for a broader study, involving a greater number of subjects and enhances the generalization of the results; it also advocates for greater objectivity and accuracy of results. Generally, quantitative methods are designed to provide summaries of data that support generalizations about the phenomena under study. In order to accomplish this, quantitative research usually involves few variables and many cases and employs prescribed procedures to ensure validity and reliability. In a nutshell, quantitative methods are presumed to have an objective approach to studying research problems where data is controlled and measured to address the accumulation of facts and to determine the causes of behaviour. As a consequence, the results of quantitative research may be statistically significant but are often humanly insignificant.

In relation to the future of quantitative methods, there is a range of issues and developments that together shape what is doable and what is seen as acceptable in terms of robust quantitative approaches to research. Amongst the most important of these are a greater awareness of methodological problems with previous approaches, ongoing methodological innovations, better computer power, greater availability of secondary and 'big' data and a stronger emphasis on demonstrating causal effects rather than just correlations in research.

End of Chapter 4 Quiz

a) Make a list of five different research problems for which quantitative method would be suitable.

b) Out of the five research problems in (a) above, pick one and then come up with a possible research hypothesis.

For the research problem you have picked in (b) above, develop five simple survey questions you might want answered by research participants and then develop simple codes for their analysis.

INTRODUCTION TO QUALITATIVE RESEARCH

"Qualitative research is an umbrella term for a wide variety of approaches to and methods for the study of natural social life."

— Johnny Saldana (2011)

Introduction

a) Qualitative research develops explanations of social phenomena and enables researchers to understand the world. Such research approach attempts to answer why people behave the way they do. Qualitative research seeks to provide answers in the following areas:

b) The manner in which people form opinions and attitudes.

c) How people perceive and react to the events that go on around them.

d) The development of cultures.

e) The distinctions that exist between social groups, and

How to get the bigger picture in a given research area.

a) Qualitative research seeks to find the answers to questions that seek justifications and manners in which events and phenomena occur. Quantitative research, on the other hand, is more concerned with questions about quantity, frequency, and degree. Other distinctive features of qualitative research are as follows:

b) Qualitative research investigates the opinions, experiences and feelings of people who are subjects of research.

c) Qualitative research seeks to describe social phenomena in their natural occurrence domains without any attempt at manipulation as is seen in experimental quantitative studies.

d) Qualitative data is collected in qualitative research in direct encounters between researchers and subjects, through one-to-one interviews, group interviews or by observation. Data collection is time consuming.

e) Qualitative research uses small samples in order to avoid intensive and time-consuming data collection procedures required for large samples.

Qualitative sampling techniques collect data from specific groups and subgroups in the population unlike quantitative techniques that seek representativeness of findings through random selection of subjects.

Qualitative Research Designs

Qualitative analysis examines qualitative data like text data from interview transcripts. Unlike quantitative analysis which relies on statistics and does not depend on the researcher, qualitative analysis relies heavily on the analytic and interpretive skills and personal knowledge the researcher has relating to the context in which data is collected. Qualitative analysis emphasizes 'sense making' and the ability to understand a phenomenon instead of explaining or predicting phenomena. Qualitative research therefore requires a creative and investigative mindset. Such a mindset needs to be pinioned on an ethically enlightened and participant-in-context attitude and a set of analytical strategies.

This session seeks to provide a glance at some of these qualitative analysis strategies as a scientific method. In general terms, scientific research consists of an investigation that seeks answers to a question, systematically uses a predefined set of procedures to answer the question, collects evidence and produces findings that were not determined in advance. It also produces findings that are applicable beyond the immediate boundaries of the study.

Theory and Research Strategies

Qualitative research is often described as an inductive strategy. Induction describes the process of constructing and validating theory using data analysis. This is to say, data analysis precedes theory construction. One methodology for qualitative and inductive theory construction is 'grounded theory' (Glaser and Strauss, 1967). Grounded theory involves working as closely as possible with the constructs used by the people who are being studied and building up from these to abstract concepts that may be linked together in qualitative models of processes or meaning systems.

Qualitative methods are generally associated with the evaluation of social dimensions. These methods provide results that are usually rich and detailed, offering ideas and concepts to inform research.

Qualitative methods can tell you how people feel and what they think, but cannot tell you how many of the target population feel or think that way as quantitative methods can (MacDonald, S. & Headlam N., 2015).

Table 1.0: Qualitative Research Strategy

Defining characteristics	Meaning-centered
Descriptive aims	Detailed descriptions of core meanings of a culture. Interpretation of the meaning of action.
Relationship between theory and research	Theory generation by means of revealing or reporting the constructions of reality in talk and text including official documents.

Defining characteristics	Meaning-centered
Epistemology	Interpretivism. The human nature of social objects requires reference to the subjective meaning when explaining social action. Theory is generated by analysis of the subjective.
Ontology	The 'social world' is constructed in our attempts to understand it and act upon it.
Theoretical perspectives	Symbolic interactionism to post-modernism. Social structure is formed by institutionalized meanings and constructs.

Qualitative research is designed to explore the human elements of a given topic, where specific methods are used to examine how individuals see and experience the world. Although qualitative research is often described in opposition to quantitative research, many scholars and practitioners are now using mixed methods and interdisciplinary approaches in their projects.

Qualitative methods are best for addressing many of the *why* questions that researchers have in mind when they develop their projects. Where quantitative approaches are appropriate for examining *who* has engaged in a behaviour or *what* has happened and while experiments can test particular interventions, these techniques are not designed to explain why certain behaviours occur. Qualitative approaches are typically used to explore new phenomena and to capture individuals' thoughts, feelings, or interpretations of meaning and process. Qualitative methods are central to research conducted in education, nursing, sociology, anthropology, information studies, and other disciplines in the humanities, social sciences and health sciences. The range of methods available is very broad (e.g., in personal interviews, observation, diaries and journals) and projects are informed by various methodologies (e.g., phenomenology, discourse analysis) and theoretical frameworks (e.g., feminist epistemology).

However, students, scholars and professionals who are new to qualitative research typically need guidance in defining the boundaries of this type of work. The guidance includes selection of specific methods, knowing what types of data are appropriate for qualitative studies, identifying theoretical frameworks for particular projects and so on. It is important that both novice and established scholars understand the language, culture, and paradigmatic approaches used in qualitative research, especially as interdisciplinary projects increasingly link researchers across varied fields of study.

Most experienced qualitative researchers will agree that if one drops a qualitative investigator into any neighbourhood, he or she will manage to identify a research idea, develop a research plan and project potential research findings. This notion is likely to contrast dramatically with the inexperienced researcher's fear that he or she cannot even think of anything worthwhile to research. There may be considerable truth to the optimistic view of experienced researchers. This does not mean, however, that all research ideas will be equally easy or interesting to research. Some ideas will be more difficult to investigate than others. This is because those who control access to a given location—what the literature calls gatekeepers or the subjects themselves may be reluctant or resistant to cooperate. From the perspective of qualitative research, non-probability sampling tends to be the norm. The following sections describe the four most common types of non-probability samples:

Convenience Samples

The convenience sample is sometimes referred to as an accidental or availability sample (Babbie, 1998; Mutchnick & Berg, 1996). This category of sample relies on available subjects—those who are close at hand or easily accessible. For example, it is fairly common for college and university professors to use their students as subjects in their research projects.

Purposive Sampling

This category of sampling is sometimes called *judgmental sampling*. When developing a purposive sample, researchers use their special knowledge or expertise about some group to select subjects who represent this population. In some instances, purposive samples are selected after field investigations on some group, in order to ensure that certain types of individuals or persons displaying certain attributes are included in the study. Despite some serious limitations (for instance, the lack of wide generalizability), purposive samples are occasionally used by researchers. Delinquent youths for example, who might not appear in sufficient numbers to be meaningful under more traditional random techniques, might be purposively sampled (Glassner et. al., 1983).

Snowball Sampling

Another non-probability sampling strategy that some may see as similar to convenience sampling is known as snowball sampling. Snowball sampling is sometimes the best way to locate subjects with certain attributes or characteristics necessary in a study. Snowball samples are particularly popular among researchers interested in studying various classes of deviance, sensitive topics or difficult to reach populations (Lee, 1993).

Quota Samples

A quota sample begins with a kind of matrix or table that creates cells or stratum. The quota sampling strategy then uses a non-probability method to fill these cells. The researcher may wish to use gender, age, education, or any other attributes to create and label each stratum or cell in the table. Which attributes are selected will have to be relevant to the research question and what study focuses on (Berg and Berg, 1993). Next, one needs to determine the proportion of each attribute in the full study population. For instance, if a researcher wanted to study perceptions of violence among people in the United States of America with a special interest in people over the age of 65, census data would provide the researcher with reasonable estimates of people in that age bracket as well as various categories under the age of 65. The researcher could create various age cohorts; people over 65, 45-65, 25-45 and under 25. Next, the researcher could determine the proportion of people in each of these age groups. Following this, the investigator could select a region of the country and sample people in that area, identifying the same proportion of people for each age cohort as identified in the census data.

When to Use Qualitative Research:

What, how, and why?

Researchers who use qualitative methods generally aim to understand the experiences and attitudes of respondents, patients, the community or health care worker. These methods aim to answer questions about the '**what**', '**how**' or '**why**' of a phenomenon rather than the '**how many**' or '**how much**', which are answered by quantitative methods.

Examples of topics that qualitative methodologies can address include:

a) People's experiences of health needs, health care, accessing care and keeping healthy.

b) Understanding different perspectives such as those of professionals and patients.

c) How experiences, attitudes and life circumstances affect health needs and behaviours.

d) New product idea generation and development.

e) Investigating current or potential product, service or brand positioning and marketing strategy.

f) Strengths and weaknesses of products or brands.

g) Understanding dynamics of purchase decision dynamics.

h) Studying reactions to advertising and public relations campaigns, other marketing communications, graphic identity or branding, package design etc.

i) Exploring market segments such as demographic and customer groups

j) Studying emotions and attitudes on societal and public affairs issues.

k) Assessing the usability of websites or other interactive products or services.

l) Understanding perceptions of a company, brand, category and product.

m) Determining consumer language as a preliminary step to develop a quantitative survey.

The Functions of Different Qualitative Methods

Social scientists argue the use of qualitative methods is heavily influenced by the aims of the research and the specific questions that need to be answered. So is the type of qualitative approach to be used to address the issues concerned. Just as qualitative and quantitative research offer different calibrations of the social world, so do different approaches and methods for collecting qualitative data (Ritchie and Lewis, 2003).

Naturally occurring data

Many of the methods used in qualitative research were developed to allow investigation of phenomena in their natural settings. They provide data which is an 'enactment' of social behaviour in its own social setting, rather than a 'recounting' of it generated specifically for the research study. They are of particular value where behaviours and interactions (whether acted, spoken or written) need to be understood in 'real world' contexts. This would be relevant for example in studies concerned with an understanding of a particular culture or community and the implicit as well as explicit tenets and 'rules' that govern it. Alternatively, naturally occurring data may be needed when the researched behaviour (Bryman, 2001) involves elements that are subconscious or instinctive, complex or delicate in their manifestation or where there are concerns about the likely veracity of participants' representations of what has occurred.

There are a number of different approaches that have been developed to study phenomena in naturally occurring settings. These include:

Participant observation in which the researcher joins the constituent study population, its organisational or community setting to record actions, interactions or events that occur. *Observation* offers the opportunity to record and analyse behaviour and interactions as they occur, although not as a member of the study population. *Documentary analysis* involves the study of existing documents, either to understand their substantive content or to illuminate deeper meanings which may be revealed by their style and coverage.

Generated data

Generated methods involve 'reconstruction' and require re-processing and re-telling of attitudes, beliefs, behaviour or other phenomena (Bryman, 2001). The experience, thought, event, behaviour or whatever, is mentally re-processed and verbally recounted by study participants. Generated data give insight into people's own perspectives on interpretation of their beliefs and behaviours, and most crucially an understanding of the meaning that they attach to them (Ibid).

Again, there are different ways in which data can be generated: *Biographical methods* use life stories, narratives and recounted biographies to understand the phenomena under study.

Individual interviews are probably the most widely used method in qualitative research. They take different forms but a key feature is their ability to provide an undiluted focus on the individual.

Focus groups or group discussions (FGDs) involve several respondents, usually somewhere between four and ten, brought together to discuss the research topic as a group.

Mixing qualitative approaches

The concept of a 'mixed method' approach to research is often discussed in the context of combining qualitative and quantitative methods. But the same principles apply to using more than one qualitative method to carry out an investigation since each brings a particular kind of insight to a study. For example, interviews are often used in combination with observation.

Conclusions

In as much as researchers will enjoy and easily adapt the research – as new patterns emerge and new data easily generated--they are also likely to be subjective and part of the research project and process. Additionally, due to the small samples used, most researchers may not be able to generalize their findings. It is, therefore, important to think through your approach to data collection and analysis thoroughly. Also, of importance is the ability to explain those choices during the data presentation phase. Although qualitative research is, in itself, sufficient enough to provide researchers with the intended results, there is always room for improvement; especially when it comes to the complimentary role that quantitative data can play.

End of Chapter 5 Quiz

i) Think of a phenomenon you have always been intrigued about and which you have been eager to find its explanation:

- Formulate the phenomenon in a scholarly manner;
- Briefly describe your tentative explanation for the phenomenon;
- Describe your possible target population and your proposed sampling method and justify your choice of this sampling method;

ii) Using concrete examples of possible application to research, distinguish between convenience sampling and purposive sampling.

iii) In line with (i) above, come up with a researchable topic.

INTRODUCTION TO MIXED METHODS RESEARCH

"A core assumption of this approach [mixed methods research] is that when an investigator combines statistical trends (quantitative data) with stories and personal experiences (qualitative data), this collective strength provides a better understanding of the research problem than either form of data alone."

— John W. Creswell (2015)

Introduction

This section provides an overview of mixed methods research. It defines the mixed research and why research uses a mixed methods approach. It also covers the foundations of mixed research and the strengths and weaknesses of mixed methods research. This is then followed by the type and the strategies of designing different types of mixed methods. The section then concludes with a brief suggestion on why mixed research is becoming the most favourable research method for social science researchers.

Defining Mixed Methods Research

Mixed methods research has come of age. To include only quantitative and qualitative methods falls short of the major approaches being used today in social and human science research. Creswell and Clark (2007) define mixed methods as "a research design with philosophical assumptions as well as methods of inquiry."

As a methodology, it involves philosophical assumptions that guide the direction of the collection and analysis of data and the mixture of qualitative and quantitative approaches in many phases in the research process. As a method, "it focuses on collecting, analysing, and mixing both quantitative and qualitative data in a single study or [a] series of studies" (Creswell and Clark, 2007:5).

The central element of each definition is that the mixed method is the use of both quantitative and qualitative approaches on one or more of the levels of epistemology, methodology and methods. Pragmatism is the philosophical underpinning for mixed method studies. Tashakkori and Teddlie (1998) and Patton (1990) convey the importance of focusing attention on the research problem in social science research, and then use pluralistic approaches to derive knowledge about the problem. For instance, pragmatism is not committed to any one system of philosophy and reality. This applies to mixed methods research in that researchers draw liberally from both quantitative and qualitative assumptions when they engage in their research. Thus, for the mixed methods researcher, pragmatism opens the door to multiple methods, different worldviews, and different assumptions, as well as to different forms of data collection and analysis in the mixed methods study.

Why Mixed Methods?

Johnson and Turner (2003) have argued that the fundamental principle of mixed methods research is that multiple kinds of data should be collected with different strategies and methods in ways that reflect complementary strengths and non-overlapping weaknesses, allowing a mixed methods study to provide insights not possible when only qualitative or quantitative data are collected. Therefore, five major purposes of (or justifications for) mixed methods over the other methods are summarized below:

a) *Triangulation:* Examines the consistency of findings, such as those obtained through different instruments, and which might include interviews and surveys. Triangulation improves the chances that threats to inferences will be controlled.

b) *Complementary:* Uses qualitative and quantitative data results to assess overlapping but distinct facets of the phenomenon under study.

c) *Development:* Results from one method influence subsequent methods or steps in the research.

d) *Initiation:* Results from one method challenge other results or stimulate new directions for the research.

e) *Expansion:* Clarifies results or adds richness to the findings.

Mixed Methods Approach: Strategies of Inquiry

The concept of mixing different methods started in 1959, when Campbell and Fiske used multiple methods to study validity of psychological traits (Ritchie and Lewis, 2003). They encouraged others to employ their "multi-method matrix" to examine multiple approaches to data collection in a study. This prompted others to mix methods and soon approaches associated with field methods such as observations and interviews (qualitative data) were combined with traditional surveys (quantitative data). Recognizing that all methods have limitations, researchers felt that biases inherent in any single method could neutralize or cancel the biases of other methods. As a result, triangulating data sources—a means for seeking convergence across qualitative and quantitative methods— were born (Jick, 1979). These reasons for mixing methods have led writers from around the world to develop procedures for mixed methods strategies of inquiry. Three general strategies and several variations within them are summarized below:

Sequential Procedures

In this method, the researcher seeks to elaborate on or expand the findings of one method with another method. This may involve beginning with a qualitative method for exploratory purposes and following up with a quantitative method with a large sample so that the researcher can generalize results to a population. Alternatively, the study may begin with a quantitative method in which theories or concepts are tested, to be followed by a qualitative method involving detailed exploration with a few cases or individuals. Creswell (2014) has further divided this method into two:

1. *Sequential explanatory design:* Qualitative data are used to enhance, complement and in some cases follow up on unexpected quantitative findings. In this approach, the focus is on interpreting and explaining relationships among variables and may or may not be guided by a particular theoretical perspective. Quantitative data is collected and analyzed first, followed by the collection and analysis of qualitative data, meaning that qualitative and quantitative data is not combined (mixed) in the data analysis; rather, integration takes place when the findings are interpreted.

2. *Sequential exploratory design*: This is essentially the reverse of the sequential explanatory design, with quantitative data used to enhance and complement qualitative results. This approach is especially useful when the researcher's interest is in enhancing generalizability, and it may or may not be guided by a theoretical perspective.

Concurrent Procedures

In this method, the researcher converges quantitative and qualitative data in order to provide a comprehensive analysis of the research problem. In this design, the investigator collects both forms of data (QUAN + QUAL) at t h e same time during the study and then integrates the information in the interpretation of the overall results. Also, in this design, the researcher nests one form of data within another in order to analyse different questions or levels of units in an organization.

1) *Concurrent triangulation design (QUAN+QAUL):* This is used when the focus is on confirming, cross-validating or corroborating findings from a single study. Qualitative and quantitative data are collected concurrently, such that the weaknesses of one kind of data are ideally offset by the strengths of the other kind. Typically,

equal weight is given to the two kinds of data in mixing the findings, although one kind of data can be weighted more heavily. The qualitative and quantitative data is analyzed separately, and mixing takes place when the findings are interpreted.

2) *Concurrent nested design (QUAN+qual or QUAL+quan):* Qualitative and quantitative data are collected concurrently and analysed together during the analysis phase. Greater weight is placed on one kind of data, in the sense that one kind of data is typically embedded in the other. However, there may or may not be a guiding theoretical perspective.

Transformative Procedures

Sequential transformative design: Either qualitative or quantitative data may be collected first. Here, the theoretical perspective underlying the methodology is critical to the conduct of the study and the chosen methods should serve the theoretical perspective. Once again, qualitative and quantitative data is analysed separately and the findings are integrated during the interpretation phase. This approach is often used to ensure that the views and perspectives of a diverse range of participants are represented or when a deeper understanding of a process that is changing as a result of being studied is sought.

Concurrent transformative design: There is a clearly defined theoretical perspective that guides the methodology. In this approach, qualitative and quantitative data are collected concurrently and can be weighted equally or unequally during the integration of findings. Qualitative and quantitative data are typically mixed during the analysis phase.

Strengths and Weaknesses of Mixed Method Research

The following are the strengths and weaknesses for mixed methods research:

Strengths:

a) Words, pictures, and narratives can be used to add meaning to numbers.

b) Numbers can be used to add precision to words, pictures and narratives.

c) The mixed method can provide quantitative and qualitative research strengths.

d) The researcher can generate and test a grounded theory.

e) Mixed method can answer a broader and more complete range of research questions because the researcher is not confined to a single method or approach.

f) In a two-stage sequential design, the stage 1 results can be used to develop and inform the purpose and design of the stage 2 component).

g) A researcher can use the strengths of an additional method to overcome the weaknesses in another method by using both in a research study.

h) Mixed method can provide stronger evidence for a conclusion through the convergence and corroboration of findings.

i) The method can add insights and understanding that might be missed when only a single method is used.

j) The method can be used to increase the generalizability of the results.

k) Qualitative and quantitative research used together produce more complete knowledge necessary to inform theory and practice.

Weaknesses

a) It can be difficult for a single researcher to carry out both qualitative and quantitative research, especially if two or more approaches are expected to be used concurrently; it may require a research team.

b) The researcher has to learn about multiple methods and approaches and understand how to mix them appropriately.

c) Methodological purists contend that one should always work within either a qualitative or a quantitative paradigm.

d) It is more expensive to use mixed method than a single method.

e) It is also more time consuming than a single method.

Some of the details of mixed research remain to be worked out fully by research methodologists (e.g., problems of paradigm mixing, how to qualitatively analyse quantitative data, how to interpret conflicting results).

Conclusions

Mixing methods is distinguished from other methodological approaches by the rigorous adherence to quality in research methods that leads to integration of qualitative and quantitative methods at the analytical and results dissemination phases. This gives access to insights and understanding beyond those that might have been provided by the use of either quantitative or qualitative methods alone. Mixed methods research is an intellectual and practical synthesis based on qualitative and quantitative research; it is the third methodological or research paradigm (along with qualitative and quantitative research).

In a nutshell, mixed methods approach recognizes the importance of traditional quantitative and qualitative research but also offers a powerful third paradigm choice that often will provide the most informative, complete, balanced, and useful research results. Growing numbers of researchers, motivated in an increasingly competitive funding climate to describe their proposed studies as methodologically novel or innovative, may consider mixed method research to be an apt choice.

End of Chapter 6 Quiz

a) Think of a phenomenon of scholarly inquiry that might require a researcher to answer both ***why*** and ***degree*** of the problem.

- Describe the phenomenon in two paragraphs of 4-5 sentences each;
- Formulate ten questions to the phenomenon and evenly split the questions between qualitative and quantitative ones;
- Identify 2-3 responses that might need triangulation.

b) What is triangulation in mixed methods research?

c) What is the significance of mixed methods in complex research projects?

RESEARCH DESIGN AND MANAGEMENT

> *"Management comes from manes, meaning 'to control by hand.' The essential meaning is to control and gain results."*
> — **Owen E. Hughes (2012)**

Introduction

The formidable problem that follows the task of defining the research problem is the preparation of the design of the research project, popularly known as the "research design." Decisions regarding **what, where, when, how much,** by **what means** concerning an inquiry or a research study constitute a research design. According to Selltiz (1959), research design is the arrangement of conditions for collection and analysis of data in a manner that aims to combine relevance to the research purpose with economy in procedure. Thus, research design is the conceptual structure within which research is conducted; it constitutes the blueprint for the collection, measurement and analysis of data. As such, the design includes an outline of what the researcher will do from writing the hypothesis and its operational implications to the final analysis of data.

More explicitly, the designing decisions happen to be in respect of:

a) what the study is about

b) why the study is being conducted

c) where the study will be carried out

d) what type of data is required

e) where the required data can be found

f) what periods of time the study will include

g) what the sample design will be

h) what techniques of data collection will be used

i) how the data will be analyzed

j) style in which the report will be prepared.

Keeping in mind the above stated design decisions, one may split the overall research design into the following parts:

a) the sampling design which deals with the method of selecting items to be observed for the given study

b) the observational design which relates to the conditions under which the observations are to be made

c) the statistical design which concerns the question of how many items are to be observed and how the information and data gathered are to be analysed

d) the operational design which deals with the techniques by which the procedures specified in the sampling, statistical and observational designs can be carried out.

Why Research Design?

Research design is needed because it facilitates the smooth sailing of the various research operations, thereby making research as efficient as possible and yielding maximal information with minimal expenditure of effort, time and money. Just as for better, economical and attractive construction of a house, we need a blueprint (or what is commonly called the map of the house) well thought out and prepared by an expert (architect).

Similarly, we need a research design or a plan in advance of data collection and analysis for our research project.

A research design stands for advance planning of the methods to be adopted for collecting the relevant data and the techniques to be used in their analysis, keeping in view the objective of the research and the availability of staff, time and money. Preparation of the research design should be done with great care as any error in it may upset the entire project. Research design, in fact, has a great bearing on the reliability of the results of research and as such constitutes the firm foundation of the entire edifice of the research work.

Even then, the need for a well thought out research design is at times not realised by many. The importance of this activity is not usually appreciated. As a result, many researches do not serve the purpose for which they are undertaken. In fact, they may even give misleading conclusions.

Thoughtlessness in designing the research project may result in rendering the whole research exercise futile. It is, therefore, imperative that an efficient and appropriate design be prepared before starting research operations. The design helps the researcher to organize the ideas in a form that makes it possible for the researcher to look for flaws and inadequacies. Such a design can even be given to colleagues or research experts for their comments and critical evaluation. In the absence of such a course of action, it will be difficult for the critic to provide a comprehensive review of the proposed study.

Features of a Good Research Design

A good design is often characterised by adjectives like flexible, appropriate, efficient, economical and so on. Generally, a good design is recognized in terms of its capacity to minimise bias and maximise the reliability of the data collected and analysed. Such a design needs to give the smallest experimental error.

Similarly, a good design should yield large quantities of data and provide ample opportunity for considering many different aspects of a problem. Thus, the question of a good design is related to the purpose or objective of the research problem and also to the nature of the problem to be studied. A design may be quite suitable in one case, but may be found wanting in one respect or the other, in the context of some other research problem. It should be noted that one single design cannot serve the purpose of all types of research problems.

If the research study happens to be an exploratory or a formulative one, the major emphasis is on the discovery of ideas and insights. The most appropriate research design must be flexible enough to permit the consideration of many different aspects of a phenomenon. But when the purpose of a study is an accurate description of a situation or of an association between variables (in what are called the descriptive studies), accuracy becomes a major consideration and a research design which minimizes bias and maximizes the reliability of the evidence collected is considered a good design.

Studies involving the testing of a hypothesis of a causal relationship between variables require a design which will permit inferences about causality in addition to the minimization of bias and maximization of reliability. But in practice, it is most difficult to put a particular study in a particular group, for a given research may have in it elements of two or more of the functions of different studies. It is only on the basis of its primary function that a study can be categorized either as an exploratory or descriptive or hypothesis-testing study and accordingly the choice of a research design may be made in case of a particular study. Besides, the availability of time, money, skills of the research staff and the means of obtaining the information must be given due weightage while working out the relevant details of the research design such as experimental design, survey design, sample design etc.

Before describing the different research designs, it will be appropriate to explain the various concepts relating to designs so that these may be better and easily understood.

a) Dependent and independent variable

A concept which can take on different quantitative values is called a variable. As such, concepts like weight, height, and income are all examples of variables. Qualitative phenomena (or the attributes) are also quantified on the basis of the presence or absence of the concerning attribute(s). Phenomena which can take on quantitatively different values even in decimal points are called continuous variables. But all variables are not continuous.

b) **Extraneous variable**

Independent variables that are not related to the purpose of the study, but may affect the dependent variable are termed as extraneous variables.

c) **Control**

One important characteristic of a good research design is to minimize the influence or effect of extraneous variable(s). The technical term 'control' is used when we design the study minimizing the effects of extraneous independent variables. In experimental researches, the term 'control' is used to refer to the act of restraining experimental conditions.

d) **Confounded relationship**

When the dependent variable is not free from the influence of extraneous variable(s), the relationship between the dependent and independent variables is said to be confounded by an extraneous variable(s).

e) **Research hypothesis**

When a prediction or a hypothesized relationship is to be tested by scientific methods, it is termed as research hypothesis. The research hypothesis is a predictive statement that relates an independent variable to a dependent variable. Usually, a research hypothesis must contain at least, one independent and one dependent variable. Predictive statements which are not to be objectively verified or the relationships that are assumed but not to be tested are not termed research hypotheses.

Different Research Designs

Different research designs can be conveniently described in the following categories as:

a) research design in case of exploratory research studies;

b) research design in case of descriptive and diagnostic research studies and,

c) research design in case of hypothesis-testing research studies.

Research Design—Exploratory Research Studies

Exploratory research studies are also termed as *formulative research studies*. The main purpose of such studies is that of formulating a problem for more precise investigation or of developing the working hypotheses from an operational point of view. The major emphasis in such studies is on the discovery of ideas and insights. As such, the research design appropriate for such studies must be flexible enough to provide opportunity for considering different aspects of a problem under study. Inbuilt flexibility in research design is needed because the research problem, broadly defined initially, is transformed into one with more precise meaning in exploratory studies, which fact may necessitate changes in the research procedure for gathering relevant data.

Research Design— Descriptive and Diagnostic Research Studies

Descriptive research studies are those studies which are concerned with describing the characteristics of a particular individual or of a group, whereas diagnostic research studies determine the frequency with which something occurs or its association with something else. The studies concerning whether certain variables are associated are examples of diagnostic research studies. As against this, studies concerned with specific predictions, with narration of facts and characteristics concerning individual, group or situation are all examples of descriptive research studies. Most of the social research comes under this category.

From the point of view of the research design, the descriptive as well as diagnostic studies share common requirements and as such, we may group together these two types of research studies. In descriptive as well as in diagnostic studies, the researcher must be able to define what to measure clearly and must find adequate methods for measuring it along with a clear-cut definition of the 'population' to be studied. Since the aim is to obtain complete and accurate information in the said studies, the procedure to be used must be carefully planned.

Research Design—Hypothesis-testing Research Studies

Hypothesis-testing research studies (generally known as experimental studies) are those where the researcher tests the hypotheses of causal relationships between variables. Such studies require procedures that will not only reduce bias and increase reliability, but will permit drawing inferences about causality. Usually experiments meet this requirement.

Research studies may want to test the hypothesis that there is a relationship between children's gains in social studies achievement and their self-concepts. In this case, self-concept is *an independent* variable and social studies achievement is a *dependent variable.* Intelligence may as well affect the social studies achievement, but since it is not related to the purpose of the study undertaken by the researcher, it will be termed as an extraneous variable.

Conclusions

There are several research designs and the researcher must decide in advance of collection and analysis of data which design would be more appropriate for his/her research project. The researcher must give due weight to various points such as the type of universe and its nature, the objective of the study, the resource list or the sampling frame, desired standard of accuracy, when taking a decision in respect of the design for the research project

End of Chapter 7 Quiz

For two years, your government has been running a social protection programme intended to cushion the elderly citizens. However, the government is unsure about the success of the programme but has received mixed feedback through suggestion boxes and other social media outlets. Your research Professor has been asked to lead a study and advise the government on the programme but the Professor is busy and has delegated the research design to your class. In groups of 3-5, come up with a full research design of this study.

DATA COLLECTION METHODS

"Times and methodologies are changing and certainly data collection technology is."— Edith D. de Leeuw (2005)

Introduction

Research normally relies on extensive data to establish the characteristics of a population. The term data comes from the Latin word *datum*, meaning that which is known. In many cases, research generates large volumes of raw data which has to be manipulated to enable researchers to make general statements and inferences on the population of interest. Data is divided into two main types depending on how it was acquired by the researcher. The two types of data are **primary data** and **secondary data.** We shall look at each of them in the following sub-sections where definitions of terms used in data collection are explained.

Raw Data

Data comes to us from the field in raw form. *Raw data* comprises numerical information that is not organized in any logical form. Often, raw scores do not have a clear relationship with other data and therefore tell us very little in terms of the population. Data from the field usually comes to researchers in this form. It is therefore the responsibility of the researcher to process the data and present it in a form that can be manipulated to understand population characteristics.

Defining Variables

A variable is a characteristic of interest in research which contains the information of interest. It is this characteristic that we manipulate to get the relevant information on phenomena. Ideally, a variable is a characteristic that has at least two values which can be measured like cost, colour or sex. Cost as a variable has values like Somali Shilling (SoSh): 10, 20, 100 and so on. We consider these values based on quantities to be *quantitative*.

Attributes are also variables which are based on characteristics like colour, sex or attitude. Colour has values like black, white, blue and so on. Sex has two values: male and female. The value of attributes is based on qualities and is therefore defined as qualitative as they mainly deal with the quality of phenomena or the presence and absence of it. We can, therefore, conclude that our population parameters come from variables and values which are either quantitative or qualitative. We shall talk about quantitative and qualitative data later. According to Kothari (2007), variables are divided into three main categories as discussed below.

a) *Independent variables:* This is the variable which causes the change that we are interested in. For instance, if the teacher's skills in research influence the attitudes of the students toward research, then the teacher's "skills" is an independent variable. We must manipulate the teacher's skills to see how it influences the students' "attitudes."

b) *Dependent variables:* We normally measure dependent variables in research in order to understand the transformations they have gone through because of the independent variable. Dependent variables are the ones we wish to explain. They are the ones affected by the independent ones. When we say that the level of income is dependent on the person's education, then, education determines your level of income which is the dependent variable.

c) *Intervening or Extraneous variables:* Extraneous variables are the unwanted variables which keep interfering or confounding our presumed relationships. These extraneous variables need to be considered and if possible controlled, to avoid spurious or unreal relationships.

Quantitative Data

Quantitative data is data that uses measurements like amount, volume, quantity and so on. The information used in quantitative research is mainly numerical and it can be used for deductive explanation and generalization for application throughout the target population.

Qualitative Data

This type of data is based on quality or attributes rather than quantity. Human behavioural characteristics are usually investigated through qualitative research. Qualitative research rarely depends on numbers other than frequencies which helps us in description. It is particularly ideal in case studies, historical and records research with no possibility for generalization. Inductive results, which apply to particular situations, rather than deductive ones, which translate into general laws of human behaviour, are sought.

Univariate Data

Univariate data is data with one variable like the age profile of students enrolled for the research methods course. The analysis of this kind of data is simple because one is essentially looking for cluster points, like the most frequent age group. In most instances, we are able to distinguish the characteristics through three sets of methods which include measures of central tendency, measures of dispersion and frequency distribution.

Bivariate Data

Bivariate data is made up of two variables. In bivariate data, the primary aim is to search for relationships or co-variation between the two variables. Relationships help us to predict one variable on the basis of the other if they are proven to be related or to co-vary. A good example is the relationship between *education* and *employment* (Johnson and Christensen, 2011).

Multivariate Data

Data containing more than two variables is usually referred to as *multivariate data*. This data is often used in research for prediction. It is mainly used for determining the possible impact of a third or more variables in a bivariate relationship. It also helps us in the elaboration of a relationship, showing how extra variables would enhance the relationship.

Sources of Data

Sources of information can be classified into primary and secondary types. Primary data comes from the original sources and are collected specifically to answer the research questions. Secondary data come from other sources, for example, other studies conducted by other persons for other purposes reports by government authorities, organizations, business enterprises, scholarly thesis, academic articles etc.

Data Collection Methods for Quantitative Research

Data Measurements

Data analysis is essentially the main stage in research. Analysis helps us to interpret data. Many methods of data analysis exist and we decide on the one(s) to use depending on the nature of the problem being investigated, the nature of data and the measurements. Here we look at four different data measurements used in quantitative research: nominal, ordinal (ranked), interval and ratio (Mugenda and Mugenda, 1999).

a) *Nominal data* is data based on name variables and values like good, bad, male, female etc. It is also referred as attribute based. A nominal variable may have numbers which have no arithmetic value. We could give numbers to attributes like female -2 and male -1 when surveying the gender of students. The numbers are mainly used for convenience and they couldbe easily replaced with symbols without affecting the results. It is considered the lowest level of measurement as the only viable statistics are frequencies and percentages.

b) *Rank (Ordinal) Data* is ordered data which follows a certain sequence. The best example is the ranking of students of the research course, where the best student is placed at the top as number 1 and the rest follow sequentially up to the last students with the lowest marks. Ordinal data is at a higher level than nominal data in terms of statistical manipulation and results and can use statistics like the Spearman's Rank Correlation Coefficient.

c) *Interval Data* is continuous information which has no clear breaks and certain rules have to be introduced in order to separate it into clear-cut interval estimates or classes. In some instances, interval data has an arbitrary starting point unlike the case in ratio data where zero is absolute. A good example is temperature where the $0°$ in Centigrade is the same as $32°$ in Farenheight. Zero may be arbitrary but the data can attract more powerful statistical analysis as the intervals are fixed and measurements are comparatively more precise than ordinal and nominal measures (Kothari, 2007).

d) *Ratio Data* with its unique absolute '0' is the highest level of data measurement. It can be manipulated using a wide array of statistical methods; almost all the statistical methods available can be used. Most measurements like distance have a zero starting point and hence the measurements are absolute. Such measures are also good for inferential statistics as they have clear-cut inequalities.

Data Collection Techniques

Data collection techniques allow us to systematically collect information about our objects of study (people, objects, phenomena) and about the settings in which they occur. In the collection of data, we have to be systematic. If data is collected haphazardly, it will be difficult to answer our research questions in a conclusive way.

Data Collection Methods for Quantitative Research

A researcher needs to decide which data collection method to use in the study. In this session, we are going to discuss the three main *data collection methods* and *data collection tools* that can be used for each method. There are many methods used to collect or obtain data for statistical analysis. Three of the most popular methods are: Surveys, Direct Observation and Experiments.

Survey Methods

To survey is to question people and record their responses for analysis. Survey method is very versatile particularly in collecting primary data. This is because it is possible to gather abstract information of all types by the survey method. Survey method is more efficient and economical than observation.

Information can be gathered by using a few well-chosen questions that would take much more time and effort by observation (Biemer and Lyberg, 2003). The major weaknesses of the survey method are:

a) the quality of information secured depends heavily on the quality and willingness of respondents to cooperate,

b) the respondents may refuse to be interviewed or fail to reply to a mail survey. Others may fear the interview experience for some personal reason or the topic may be too sensitive, at the same time, the respondents may not have the knowledge required on the topic,

c) the respondents may also interpret a question or concept differently from what was intended by the researcher,

d) the respondents may intentionally mislead the researcher by giving false information.

Notwithstanding these weaknesses, the survey method is widely used in research in all fields. **A survey method is most appropriate where the respondents are uniquely qualified to provide the desired information.** There are three main techniques that can be used to get information using the survey methods:

a) *Personal interview/key informant interview:* A personal interview (i.e., face to face) is a two-way conversation initiated by an interviewer to obtain information from the respondent. This technique is deeper and detailed in terms of the information collected. The interviewer has more control than other kinds of interrogation, and the interviewer can adjust to the language of the interviewee because they can observe the problems and effects the interview is having on the respondent. However, it is relatively expensive and interviewers are usually reluctant to visit unfamiliar neighbourhoods alone. In addition, the results can be affected adversely by interviewers who alter the questions asked. The main characteristics of personal interviews are:

- The roles of the interviewer and respondents are very different. They are both strangers and the interviewer generally controls the engagement.
- The consequences of the interviewing event are usually insignificant for the respondent.
- The respondent is asked to provide information with little hope of receiving any immediate or direct benefit from this cooperation.

b) *Telephone interview:* This is a technique by which the data is collected by telephoning the respondents. It is a good technique particularly with unusual types of respondents. It is relatively cheaper and responses are received immediately and the study comes to a faster completion. However, phone interview has its own limitations. For instance, the respondent must be available by phone. The discussion is relatively limited because of the time one can spend on a telephone line. Telephone interviews can result in less thorough responses and that those interviewed by phone find the experience less rewarding to them than a personal interview (Groves, 1990).

c) ***Mail interview/self-administered questionnaires:*** Mail survey or self- administered questionnaires is a technique of data collection in which the respondent completes surveys at their convenience. They are usually delivered by mail to the respondent (Dillman, 2003). The mail interview has several advantages including:

- They typically cost less than the personal interviews. The more dispersed the sample, the more likely it will be the low-cost method.
- By using mail, it is possible to get to the respondents who can otherwise be inaccessible.
- The mail allows the respondent to take more time to collect facts, talk to others or consider replies at length than is possible with the telephone or personal interview.
- A mail survey is perceived as more impersonal, hence providing more anonymity than the other communication modes. However, the mail interview or self-administered questionnaires are associated with a high rate of non-response. This makes it difficult to know how the answers of those who respond are different from those who do not answer. In most cases, the respondents do not provide adequate information. Usually, there are many questions that are never answered.

The Experimental Method

Experiments are studies involving intervention by the researcher beyond that required for measurement. This intervention involves the manipulation of some variables in a setting and observing how they affect the subjects being studied. The researcher manipulates the independent or explanatory variable and then observes whether the hypothesised dependent variable is affected by the intervention (Johnson and Christensen, 2011).

The level of the independent variable is the distinction the researcher makes between different aspects of the treatment conditions. The levels assigned to an independent variable should be based on simplicity and common sense. There are two main levels: *the control group* and *the experimental treatment group* (Balnaves and Caputi, 2001).

The control group: This group provides a base level for comparison. It is composed of subjects who are not exposed to the independent variable. No treatment is provided to this group.

The experimental group: This is the group to which treatment is provided. This is the group upon which the independent variable is manipulated.

A researcher must be judicious in selecting the experimental design to employ. There are several designs that can be used. They are:

a) ***Pre-experimental design:*** This is divided into three types:
- The one-shot case study: This is a case in which there is treatment or manipulation of independent variable and observation or measurement is done on the dependent variable.
- The one-group pre-test, post-test design: In this case we have a pre-test (O), manipulation (X), post-test (o).
- The Static Group Comparison which provides for two groups; one which receives the experimental treatment while the other serves as a control.

b) ***True experimental designs (laboratory experiment):*** The essential ingredients of a true experimental design are that subjects are randomly assigned to the treatment group.

c) ***Field experiments:*** In comparison with laboratory design, the field experiments research takes place in a natural situation and the investigator manipulates one or more independent variables under conditions that are carefully controlled as the situation permits. If an experimental study was to be conducted in the field, we often cannot control enough of the extraneous variables or the experimental treatment to use a true experimental design. In this case we use the field experiment.

Data Collection Techniques for Qualitative Research

In-Depth Interviewing

The in-depth interview is a technique designed to elicit a vivid picture of the participant's perspective on the research topic. During in-depth interviews, the person being interviewed is considered the expert and the interviewer is considered the student. The researcher's interviewing techniques are motivated by the desire to learn everything the participant can share about the research topic (Groves, 1990).

Researchers engage with participants by posing questions in a neutral manner, listening attentively to participants' responses and asking follow-up questions and probes based on those responses. They neither lead participants according to any preconceived notions, nor encourage participants to provide particular answers by expressing approval or disapproval of what they say.

In-depth interviews are usually conducted face-to-face and involve one interviewer and one participant. When safety is an issue for the interviewer, the presence of two interviewers is appropriate. In these situations, however, care must be taken not to intimidate the participant. Phone conversations and interviews with more than one participant also qualify as in-depth interviews, but, in this module, we focus on individual, face-to-face interviews.

Why Use In-depth Interviews?

In-depth interviews are useful for learning about the perspectives of individuals. They are an effective qualitative method for getting people to talk about their personal feelings, opinions, and experiences. They are also an opportunity for us to gain insight into how people interpret and order the world. We can accomplish this by being attentive to the causal explanations that participants provide for what they have experienced and what they believe. By actively probing them about the connections and relationships, they distinguish between particular events, phenomena and beliefs. Interviews are also especially appropriate for addressing sensitive topics that people might be reluctant to discuss in a group setting.

Focus Group Discussions (FGDs)

Focus group discussions are a qualitative data collection method effective in helping researchers learn the social norms of a community or subgroup, as well as the range of perspectives that exist within that community or subgroup. Focus groups are often used to determine what service or product a particular population wants or would like to have, such as in marketing studies. Because focus groups seek to illuminate group opinion, the method is especially well suited for socio-behavioural research that will be used to develop and measure services that meet the needs of a given population. A focus group is a small group of six to ten people, led through an open discussion by a skilled moderator. The group needs to be large enough to generate rich discussions but not so large as to leave out some participants. Depending on the research objective, the focus group discussion can be used alone or in conjunction with other methods. The results obtained from the FGD application are particularly effective in supplying information about how people think, feel, or act regarding a specific topic (Freitas et. al., 1998).

A focus group discussion is a qualitative data collection method in which one or two researchers and several participants meet to discuss a given research topic. These sessions are usually tape-recorded or sometimes, videotaped. One researcher (the moderator) leads the discussion by asking participants to respond to open-ended questions; that is, questions that require an in-depth response rather than a single phrase or simple "yes" or "no" answer. A second researcher (the note-taker) takes detailed notes of the discussion.

The principal advantage of focus groups is that they yield a large amount of information over a relatively short period of time. They are also effective for accessing a broad range of views on a specific topic, as opposed to achieving group consensus. Focus groups are not the best method for acquiring information on highly personal or socially sensitive topics. One-on-one interviews are better-suited for such topics.

Strengths of Focus Groups versus In-depth Interviews

The table below summarizes some of the strengths of focus groups in comparison to in-depth interviews (Groves, 1990).

	Appropriate for:	Strength of method
Focus groups	Identifying group norms Eliciting opinions about group norms Discovering variety within a population	Elicits information on a range of norms and opinions in a short time Group dynamic stimulates conversation, reactions
Interviews	Eliciting individual experiences, opinions, feelings Addressing sensitive topics	Elicits in-depth responses, with nuances and contradictions Gets at interpretive perspective, i.e., the connections and relationships a person sees between particular events, phenomena, and beliefs

The Observation Method

Observation as a method of data collection involves the five human senses, vision, hearing, touching, smelling and tasting. Observation method is also defined as a technique that involves systematically selecting, watching and recording behaviour and characteristics of living beings, objects or phenomena. Without training, our observations will heavily reflect our personal choices of what to focus on and what to remember. You need to heighten your sensitivity to details that you would normally ignore and at the same time, be able to focus on phenomena of true interest to your study.

When used in scientific research, observation includes the full range of monitoring behavioural and non-behavioural activities and conditions, which can be classified as follows, according to Rosenbaum (2005):

a) **Behaviour Observation:** This is further classified into: *Nonverbal analysis* which includes body movement, motor expressions, and exchange of glances and cues. *Linguistic analysis* refers to the manifest content of speech and various attributes of verbal communication. *Extra-linguistic analysis* includes the communication attributes like the vocal, temporal, interactional and verbal stylistics. *Spatial analysis* refers to the attempt of individuals to structure the physical space around them. This includes how a person relates physically to others.

b) **Non-behaviour Observation:** This is further classified into: *Record analysis* which involves historical or current records and public or private records. *Physical condition analysis* which involves analysis of, say, inventories, financial statements, plant safety compliance etc. *Physical process analysis* which includes the analysis of processes like traffic flow, distribution systems, banking system etc.

Dimensions of Observation

1. Space (physical places)

2. Actors (people involved)
3. Activities (the set of related acts people do)
4. Object (the physical things that are present)
5. Time (the sequencing that takes place over time)
6. Goal (the things people are trying to accomplish)
7. Feeling (the emotions felt and expressed

Preparing for Observation

i) Determine the purpose of the observation activity as related to the overall research objectives.

ii) Determine the population(s) to be observed.

iii) Consider the accessibility of the population(s) and the venues in which you would like to observe them.

iv) Investigate possible sites for participant observation and preparing for observation.

v) Select the site(s), time(s) of day, and date(s), and anticipate how long you will collect participant observation data on each occasion.

vi) Decide how field staff will divide up or pair off to cover all sites most effectively.

vii) Consider how you will present yourself, both in terms of appearance and how you will explain your purpose to others if necessary as you are preparing for observation.

viii) Plan how and if you will take notes during the participant observation activity.

ix) Remember to take your field notebook and a pen after participant observation.

x) Schedule time soon after participant observation to expand your notes.

xi) Type your notes into computer files using the standard format set for the study.

How to Conduct an Observational Study

We have two types of observational studies:

a) *Simple observation:* Its practice is not standardised because of the discovery nature of the exploratory research where it is often used.

b) *Systematic observation:* It employs standardised procedures, trained observers' schedules for recording and other devices for the observer that mirror the scientific procedures of other primary data methods (Rosenbaum, 2005).

In the observation method, we need to answer the following questions if we are to gather the required data. Who are the targets? Who qualifies to be observed? What is to be observed? (The characteristics of the observation must be set in terms of elements and units of analysis). When is the observation to take place? (That is whether the time of the study is important or whether the study can take place any time). How will the data be observed? If there is more than one observer, how shall they divide the observation task? How shall the results be recorded for later analysis? How shall the observers deal with various situations that may occur?

Conclusions

Research scholars often examine the main components of a research framework; from the statement of the research problem, the research design, data collection and analysis, as well as ethical issues that may arise while carrying out their research, report writing and presentation. While undertaking research, it is noteworthy that, no single method of data collection is, in itself, sufficient enough to answer all research questions. For maximum benefits, however, researchers use combined data collection techniques of both quantitative and qualitative research methods when using mixed methods research. For instance, a researcher can use self-administered questionnaires for the quantitative component of the study and in-depth interviews for the qualitative component of the study.

End of Chapter 8 Quiz

a) For each of the following levels of measurement of data, give three examples.

i) *Ordinal ii) nominal iii) ratio iv) interval*

For example: Data about students' admission numbers is <u>nominal</u> level of measurement.

b) Go back to the quiz in Chapter 5, from the phenomenon you identified:

- What is the dependent variable?
- What is the independent variable?
- Think of a possible extraneous variable to the research?

c) Think of a research experiment in the social sciences that you might want to do. In 3 paragraphs, describe the research, its control and treatment groups.

CHAPTER 09
DATA ANALYSIS AND INTERPRETATION

> *"It is time now to worry about something that has been implicit throughout the discussion of methodology...those mysterious procedures by which you transform what you see and hear into intelligible accounts."*
>
> — **Michael H. Agar (1980)**

Introduction

Data analysis refers to the computation of certain measures along with searching for patterns of relationships that exist among datagroups. In the process of analysis, relationships or differences supporting or conflicting with original or new hypothesis should be subjected to statistical tests of significance to determine with what validity data can be said to indicate any conclusions. Data analysis is essentially one of the main stages in research. Analysis helps us in interpreting data, drawing conclusions and making decisions. In descriptive statistics, we are able to present our findings in a concise manner and in inferential statistics; we are able to develop generalizations from the sample to the population.

Many methods of data analysis are available and our decision to use any of them depends on the nature of the problem being investigated, the nature of data, the measurements used and the level of precision required among many other considerations. This session covers the main processing methods which are; *editing, coding* and *re-coding, tabulation* and *classification*. Using Balnaves and Caputi (2003), we will also discuss the basic methods of data presentation and also look at the different methods used in the manipulation of univariate and bivariate analysis and relationships.

Data Processing and Presentation

Data Editing and Coding

Data editing involves some level of proof-reading which eliminates common mistakes. It can be done in the field or in a more centralized environment like the researcher's office when field work is complete. At this stage, it is possible to eliminate common problems like duplication of information, vague responses and other information that might interfere with the outcome of the computer analysis. Another aspect of editing is data cleaning which is a variation of proof- reading that also helps in ensuring consistency in data and coding processes. This process is crucial because errant values can be arrested long before they interfere with the results.

Data coding is the process in which variables are illustrated in the form of symbols or numeric characters. This helps to reduce the amount of data entry required particularly where the information sought comprises attributes.

Data Presentation

Data presentation is a tool through which observed data can be summarized to give a visual impression of the distribution. This makes it easy for the reader to see the differences more clearly. Visual data representation can take many different forms but the most common forms are:

a) Percentages
b) Tables
c) Histograms
d) Bar charts
e) Frequency polygons, and
f) Pie charts.

Quantitative Data Analysis

Broadly speaking, data analysis falls into two categories namely; *descriptive* and *inferential* analysis. Descriptive analysis describes the phenomena in statistical terms as it happens or in an *ex- post-facto* sense. No attempts are made to make predictions or inferences. It helps us summarize data and manipulate it with ease (Muijs, 2004). Inferential data analysis moves a notch higher by drawing implications from hypothesis testing and making estimations or inferences in terms of theory. The ultimate aim is to come up with general laws that explain the phenomena of interest on the basis of a sample. What happens to the sample can be applied anywhere else on earth where the population bears the same characteristics of interest (Gorard, 2003).

Data comes to us as ratio, ordinal, nominal and interval. These measurements have an impact on how data is analyzed and the reliability of the conclusions reached. Ratio data, with its absolute '0', can be manipulated using a wide array of methods while nominal data is comparatively weaker.

Descriptive Statistics

Descriptive statistics are very basic methods of data analysis which are associated with the distribution of univariate data. They are: *measures of central* tendency, which deal with single value summaries and *measures of dispersion*, which compute the spread of values relative to their *mean, mode* or *median*.

a) *Measures of Central Tendency*

Measures of central tendency comprise mean, mode and median. These are single summary points also known as cluster points which reduce data into single values. The single values are supposed to give us the whole story. They normally ignore the distribution of individual values. Arithmetic *Mean* is the value that results from dividing the total value in a distribution by the total number of items. *Mode* represents the highest value or most frequent value in a distribution. *Median* is the value of the middle item in a sequential distribution and is normally known as a median. Median normally divides the distribution into two equal parts; one part being higher than the median and the other lower than it (Kothari, 2004).

b) *Measures of Dispersion*

Measures of dispersion deal with variations in the distribution of data i.e. they measure variability within data. Measures of dispersion vary considerably from the measures of central tendency. The latter depends on single cluster points while in the former, each value is weighted against the mean, mode or median to determine its distribution from the centre either negatively or positively.

Most researchers compute deviation from the mean. The mostcommonly used measures of dispersion are:

i) *Range* which computes the spread of data from the lowest to the highest number. It is essentially the difference between extreme values.

ii) *Mean deviation* is made up of deviation of the sum of scores from the mean arrived at by subtracting the mean from the observed scores.

iii) *Standard deviation* is a widely used measure of dispersion. The standard deviation is generated by squaring the mean deviation and computing the square root. The figure generated gives us an indication of the variation between observed values. The standard deviation is an important measure in the computation of parametric data, where values of a univariate variable are assumed to take a particular shape known as a normal curve or bell- s h a p e d curve (also known as normal distribution curve).

iv) *Variance* is the average square of the deviation of measurements about their mean (Balnaves and Caputi, 2001; Kothari 2004).

Summary of Central Tendencies and Variability

Univariate Statistics	Variables	Description
Mode	Nominal, Ordinal and Interval	Most frequent category or value
Median	Ordinal and Interval	Category or value that lies in the middle
Mean	Interval	Value that represents the average

Univariate Statistics	Variables	Description
Range	Interval	Highest value minus lowest value
Standard Deviation	Interval	On average how much each individual value is dispersed around the mean
Variance	Interval	Standard deviation squared

Inferential Statistics

a) *Comparing Two or More Groups*

The following methods are used if a researcher is interested in comparing differences in two or more group means and determining whether the difference is statistically significant or a result of sampling error. This portion will provide a table of some of the differences between the methods and a brief discussion of important details as it also clarifies the methods (Mugenda and Mugenda, 2003).

Method of Analysis	Summary Description
(1) Two sample T Test	Two sample t test compares means across TWO (and only two) groups. For instance, a researcher wishes to know if there is a difference in the amount of sales (in shillings) between company A and company B.
(2) Paired T Test	Paired t (also referred to as matched t) test compares means across the same variable and the same cases at two different times. Suppose you were interested in looking to see if training was effective. You had data on the data of exam test before the training was implemented and exam result after training.

Method of Analysis	Summary Description
(3) Analysis of Variance (ANOVA)	Analysis of Variance (ANOVA) is similar to the two sample t test, but it compares means across more than two groups. A researcher would use ANOVA if he/she was interested in comparing the difference in the amount of sales (in shillings) between company A, company B and company C.

b) *Measure of Relationship*

Measures of relationship represent a higher level of analysis compared to the preceding measures of central tendency and measures of dispersion. The characteristics of this kind of analysis are primarily meant to establish co-variation i.e., change and direction of the change in variables of interest. The assumption is that for every measurement (value) in one variable (y) there is a corresponding value for the second variable (x). There are a number of ways in which the relationship can be tested (Kothari, 2004).

Method of Analysis	Summary Description
1) Regression analysis	The cause and effect relationships can be measured using the linear regression analysis. Predictions can also be made. Simple regression analysis presents the relationship between an independent variable and a dependent variable. In multiple linear regressions, we look at the relationship between one 'effect' variable, called *the dependent* or *outcome variable*, and one or more predictors, also called *independent variables*. As with most other methods, a number of conditions need to be met before we can use regression analysis with confidence. The two most important conditions are that: i) the relationship between independent and dependent variables must be linear, ii) the independent variables shouldn't be too strongly correlated to one another. These conditions can be confirmed by testing the linearity, outliers and multicollinearity of the data.

Method of Analysis	Summary Description
2) Pearson's Moment Product Correlation	In the Pearson's product moment correlation, we are interested in the degree of scatter in a relationship and its strength. The less scattered the variables, the stronger the relationship. We use **"r"** to represent the product moment coefficient. The value of **"r"** lies between **-1** and **+1**. If the correlation is positive and the points lie in a straight line with a value of 1, then we call this a perfect positive correlation. This means that Pearson's **'r'** gives us information about a number of aspects of the relationship: *i)* the direction of the relationship: a positive sign indicates a positive direction (high scores on **X** means high scores on **Y),** a negative sign indicates a negative direction (high score on **X means** low scores on **Y)** *ii) the* strength of the relationship: the closer to **1** (+ or −) the stronger the relationship.

Qualitative Data Analysis

Process of Data Analysis

The mass of words generated by interviews or observational data needs to be described and summarized. The question may require the researchers to seek relationships between various themes that have been identified, to relate behaviour or ideas to biographical characteristics of respondents such as age or gender. Analysis of qualitative data usually goes through some or all of the following stages, though the order may vary (Ritchie and Lewis, 2003):

a) Familiarization with the data through review, reading, listening etc.
b) Transcription of tape-recorded material.
c) Organization and indexing of data for easy retrieval and identification.
d) Anonymising of sensitive data.
e) Coding (may be called indexing).

f) Identification of themes.
g) Re-coding.
h) Development of provisional categories.
i) Exploration of relationships between categories.
j) Refinement of themes and categories.
k) Development of theory and incorporation of pre-existing knowledge.
l) Testing of theory against the data.
m) Report writing, including excerpts from original data if appropriate (e.g. quotes from interviews).

Qualitative Data Analysis Techniques

Leech and Onwuegbuzie (2008) conceptualized that the following 17 qualitative data analysis techniques can be used to analyze literature: constant comparison analysis, keywords-in context, word count, classical content analysis, domain analysis, taxonomic analysis, componential analysis, theme analysis, discourse analysis, secondary data analysis, membership categorization analysis, narrative analysis, qualitative comparative analysis, semiotics, manifest content analysis, text mining, and micro-interlocutor analysis.

The summary definition of the data analysis techniques is presented below:

Table 1. Possible Qualitative Analyses for Research

Type of Analysis	Short Description of Analysis
Constant comparison analysis	Systematically reducing source(s) to codes inductively, then developing themes from the codes. These themes may become headings and subheadings in the literature review section
Classical content analysis	Systematically reducing source(s) to codes deductively or inductively, then counting the number of codes

Type of Analysis	Short Description of Analysis
Word count	Counting the total number of (key)words used or the number of times a particular word is used either during a within-study or between-study literature analysis
Keywords-in-context	Identifying keywords and utilizing the surrounding words to understand the underlying meaning of the keyword in a source or across sources.
Domain analysis	Utilizing the relationships between symbols and referents to identify domains in a source(s).
Taxonomic analysis	Creating a classification system that categorizes the domains in a pictorial representation (e.g., flowchart) to help the literature reviewer understand the relationships among the domains.
Componential analysis	Using matrices and/or tables to discover the differences among the subcomponents of domains.
Theme analysis	Involves a search for relationships among domains, as well as a search for how these relationships are linked to the overall cultural context.
Discourse analysis	Selecting representative or unique segments of language use, such as several lines of an interview transcript involving a researcher, and then examining the selected lines in detail for rhetorical organization, variability, accountability, and positioning. This analysis is particularly useful when reviewing literature review sections of empirical articles, literature review articles, theoretical/conceptual articles, and methodological articles.

Type of Analysis	Short Description of Analysis
Secondary data analysis	Analyzing pre-existing sources or artifacts.
Membership categorization analysis	Examining how authors/researchers communicate research terms, concepts, findings, and categories in their works.
Semiotics	Using talk and text as systems of signs under the assumption that no meaning can be attached to a single term. This form of analysis shows how signs are interrelated for the purpose of creating and excluding specific meanings.
Manifest content analysis	Describing observed (i.e., manifest) aspects of communication via objective, systematic, and empirical means.
Qualitative comparative analysis	Systematically analysing similarities and differences across sources, typically being used as a theory-building approach, allowing the reviewer to make connections among previously built categories, as well as to test and to develop the categories further. This analysis is particularly useful for assessing causality in findings across sources.
Narrative analysis	Considering the potential of stories to give meaning to research findings, and treating data as stories, enabling reviewers to reduce data to a summary.
Text mining	Analysing naturally occurring texts within multiple sources in order to discover and capture semantic information.

Type of Analysis	Short Description of Analysis
Micro-interlocutor analysis	Analysing information stemming from one or more focus groups of researchers, scholars, or practitioners about which participant(s) responds to each question, the order in which each participant responds, the characteristics of the response, the nonverbal communication used etc.

Table 1 presents the 17 qualitative data analysis techniques categorized by the four source types (i.e., talk, observations, drawings/photographs/videos and documents).

Table 2: Relationship between Sources of Information for Research and Type of Qualitative Data Analysis Technique

Source of Information	Type of Qualitative Technique
Talk	Discourse Analysis Narrative Analysis Semiotics Qualitative Comparative Analysis Constant Comparison Analysis Keywords-in-Context Word Count Membership Categorization Analysis Domain Analysis Taxonomic Analysis Componential Analysis Theme Analysis Classical Content Analysis

Source of Information	Type of Qualitative Technique
Observations	Qualitative Comparative Analysis Constant Comparison Analysis Keywords-in-Context Word Count Domain Analysis Taxonomic Analysis Componential Analysis Theme Analysis Manifest Content Analysis
Drawings/ Photographs/ Video	Qualitative Comparative Analysis Constant Comparison Analysis Word Count Manifest Content Analysis Secondary Data Analysis
Documents	Semiotics Qualitative Comparative Analysis Constant Comparison Analysis Keywords-in-Context Word Count Secondary Data Analysis Domain Analysis Taxonomic Analysis Componential Analysis Theme Analysis Classical Content Analysis Text Mining

Use of Computer-Assisted Qualitative Data Analysis Software

Computer-Assisted Qualitative Data Analysis Software (**CAQDAS**) is useful for coding data, disaggregating it into manageable components and identifying or naming these segments. Emerging concepts, categories and themes can be easily coded, recoded or edited throughout the entire process. It is important to understand that in qualitative research, software programmes cannot do the analysis by themselves—not with the same output expectations of **S**tatistical **P**ackage for **S**ocial **S**ciences **(SPSS)** or **S**tatistical **A**nalysis **S**ystem **(SAS)**. The software will not read the text and decide what it means; the researcher is still the main tool for analysis (Weitzman 2000). The software may provide tools to help analyse. Nevertheless, the researcher must learn data analysis methods (Leech and Onwuegbuzie, 2007).

According to Weitzman (2000), a software programme can be used to facilitate analysis in the following ways:

Making Notes	Performing Content Analysis	Drawing and Verifying Conclusions
Writing Up	Displaying Data	Building Theory
Editing	Writing Reports	Mapping Data Graphically
Coding	Storing Data	
Searching And Retrieving Data	Data 'Linking'	Memo-ing

Presenting the Data

Research findings will eventually be presented to a wider audience, typically in written format. Specific to theoretical approach, results could take the following forms:

a) A chronological narrative of an individual's life (narrative research),
b) A detailed description of an experience (phenomenology),
c) A theory generated from the data (grounded theory),
d) A detailed portrait of a culture-sharing group (ethnography), or
e) An in-depth analysis of one or more cases (case study) (Creswell 2009, 193).

The results of a qualitative study should include themes derived from the data, a thorough description of the themes and multiple perspectives from participants or detailed descriptions of the settings or individuals to support these themes.

Conclusions

Quantitative analysis approaches are particularly helpful when the qualitative information has been collected in some structured way, even if the actual information has been elicited through participatory discussions and approaches. Quantitative and qualitative information falls upon a continuum and varies according to the type of data, collection tool and method of data analysis. The main distinction between the two is that qualitative methods do not seek statistical significance and thus, cannot be extrapolated without relying on judgment. Any extrapolation of qualitative data to larger areas will inevitably be general and not statistically rigorous. Qualitative research methods make up for lack of statistical rigour by providing explanations and understanding.

End of Chapter 9 Quiz

a) Explain 3 reasons why data editing is important after conducting research.

b) Go back to the quiz at the end of Chapter 6 and code each of the 10 research questions.

c) For each of the following descriptive statistics, describe a suitable application:
- Median
- Range
- Standard Deviation

CHAPTER 10
RESEARCH PROPOSAL WRITING

"Writing a research proposal is a source of anxiety for most students who may feel lost in [the] face of the novelty of the process, pressured by time restrictions and stressed by the forthcoming evaluation of their work."

— **Anthony J. Onwuegbuzie (1997)**

Introduction

Research is defined as a scientific and systematic search for pertinent information on a specific topic. Kothari (1990) defines research as a systematized effort to gain new knowledge. According to Wellington et al (2005), however, academic research comprises defining and redefining problems, formulating hypotheses or suggesting solutions; collecting, organizing and evaluating data; making deductions and reaching conclusions; and at last, carefully testing the conclusions to determine whether they fit the formulated hypotheses.

According to Kothari (2004), the purpose for carrying out research is, *first* to gain familiarity with a phenomenon or to achieve new insights into it as in the case of exploratory or formulative research studies. The *second* objective is to portray the characteristics of a particular individual, situation or a group accurately, as in the case of descriptive research studies. *Third*, research is often carried out to determine the frequency with which something occurs or with which it is associated with something else, as in the case of diagnostic research studies. *Lastly*, research seeks to test a hypothesis of a causal relationship between variables, as in the case of hypothesis-testing research studies (Ibid.).

Types of Research

Kothari (2004) identifies four major types of research; they include: a) applied vs fundamental research, b) descriptive vs analytical research c) quantitative vs qualitative research, d) conceptual vs empirical research.

First, applied research aims at finding a solution for an immediate problem facing a society, an industry, a business, or an organisation. For instance, research is aimed at identifying social, economic or political trends that may affect a particular institution. Fundamental research is mainly concerned with generalizations and with the formulation of a theory. An example is research studies concerning human behaviour carried on with a view to making generalisations about human behaviour.

Descriptive research, also known as *ex post facto* research, is that which includes surveys and fact-finding enquiries of different kinds. The major purpose of descriptive research is the description of the state of affairs as it exists at present. In this case, the researcher has no control over the variables; s/he can only report what has happened or what is happening. The methods of research utilized in descriptive research are survey methods of all kinds like research on the frequency of shopping and preferences of people. In analytical research, the researcher has to use facts or information already available, and analyse these to make a critical evaluation of the material (Kothari, 2004).

Quantitative research is based on the measurement of quantity or amount. It is applicable to phenomena that can be expressed in terms of quantity. Qualitative research is concerned with the qualitative phenomenon, i.e., phenomena relating to or involving quality or kind. This type of research is especially important in the behavioural sciences where the aim is to discover the underlying motives of human behaviour. Through such research we can analyse the various factors which motivate people to behave in a particular manner or which make people like or dislike a particular thing (Kothari, 2004).

Conceptual research is the type related to some abstract idea(s) or theory. It is generally used by philosophers and thinkers to develop new concepts or to reinterpret existing ones. On the other hand, empirical research relies on experience or observation alone, often without due regard for system and theory. It is data-based research, coming up with conclusions which are capable of being verified through observation or experiment. Evidence gathered through experiments or empirical studies is today considered to be the most powerful support possible for a given hypothesis (Kothari, 2004).

Criteria for Good Research

According to Bellenger and Barnett (2014), good research should *first* be systematic. In this case, it should be structured with specified steps to be taken in a specified sequence in accordance with the well-defined set of rules. *Second,* it should be logical; this implies that research is guided by the rules of logical reasoning and the logical process of induction and deduction are of great value in carrying out research. *Third, it* should be empirical; in this case, research is related basically to one or more aspects of a real situation and deals with concrete data that provides a basis for external validity to research results. *Lastly,* it should be replicable to allow research results to be verified by replicating the study and thereby building a sound basis for decisions (Bellinger and Barnett, 1978).

Proposal Writing

Proposal writing is the first step at producing a thesis or a major project in research. It is often written in the future tense. The proposal is expected to *first,* show that the writer has engaged in genuine investigation in a bid to find out about something worthwhile in a particular context. *Secondly,* it seeks to relate the writer's planned work with the work of other writers, while at the same time proving the writer acquaintance with major schools of thought relevant to their topic of study. *Thirdly,* it proposes to establish adherence to a particular theoretical orientation, the writer's methodological approach, and lastly shows that the writer has thought about the ethical issues.

According to Procter, University of Toronto's Writing Support programme, the proposal intends to convince the supervisor or academic committee that the writer's topic and approaches are sound, so that one may gain approval to proceed with the actual research. It is a combination of the background study, literature review and research methodology. It introduces the research problem, purpose and significance of the study, research questions and hypotheses, explanation of the theory that is guiding the study and a review of relevant literature. It is often written using the Chicago Manual of Style (CMS).

The Structure of a Research Proposal

The Topic and the Title—Before researchers come up with a topic, they should find the problem and formulate it so that it becomes susceptible to research. Ackoff defines a research problem as some difficulty which a researcher experiences in the context of either a theoretical or practical situation and wants to obtain a solution for the same (Ackoff, 1961). Kothari advises that too narrow or too vague problems should be avoided; a subject selected for research should be familiar and feasible so that the related research material or sources of research are within one's reach and that overdone subjects should not be chosen, for they will be a difficult task to get new knowledge on (Kothari, 2004).

From the research problem, one will be able to come up with a topic, a n d then a title for their research. The selected topic should be concise and descriptive. Often, titles are stated in terms of a functional relationship, because such titles clearly indicate the independent and dependent variables. However, if possible, think of an informative but catchy title. An effective title not only pricks the reader's interest, but also predisposes him or her favourably towards the proposal.

Introduction—Every chapter must begin with an introduction. This is an overview of the subject area/matter of the research. It is a brief overview, the overall objective of the study and ends with some of the hypothetical debates/arguments the study contends and/or some of the key findings the study may probably come up with. The introduction should highlight key contents of the chapter and provide concise and sequential details of specific content areas.

Background to the Study—This section must contextualise the research issue and culminate into the research problem statement (Kothari, 2004). It answers the question **WHAT**? It also focuses on the historical, cultural, political, social or organizational information about the context of the research. It may also include a theoretical starting point or policy, personal motivation or problematise the status quo. It is a bit historical and it mainly focuses on how much your audience should know about the study area. For the purpose of research at university, the audience is the academia, policy-makers as well as members of the policy community. In a nutshell, a research proposal is a presentation of the need for the research including a historical background of the subject under study.

Statement of the Research Problem—In this section, the researcher should problematise the research. The problem should be stated in a broad general way, keeping in view either some practical concern or some scientific or intellectual interest. Then the researcher should narrow it down and phrase the problem in operational terms. A problem statement points out the precise gap that exists in the literature, theory or practice which the particular research will address. It entails a logical argument generated from preceding facts as articulated in the background section.

Researchers should avoid in-text referencing characterised by cut-and- paste from the background section. The key guiding question is a paraphrase of the research topic, this should be specific to the problem being addressed and supported by some literature to justify the reason for the study. Note that the problem should be clearly identified as a gap that needs to be addressed. The statement of the problem should also end with a key guiding question (KGQ).

Objectives of the Study—Researchers should have one broad objective, mainly a paraphrase of the topic again and then break it down to three or four specific ones. It is a breakdown of the purpose of the study into specific measurable tasks. The objectives should be between three and four. They should answer the questions **What, How, Why, or What**

if? They should be few so that the focus is manageable. The aims will be related to the purpose and the questions.

Research Questions—Research questions address the key concerns that guide the study. The difference between research questions and objectives is that a research question is stated in a question form while an objective is a statement. Since the two are closely related, a research proposal can either have objectives or research questions and not both; unless the objectives are broader and the research questions are more specific (Mugenda and Mugenda, 2003).

Hypotheses—The study should propose at least three (3) testable hypotheses which should be presented in bullet points. Hypotheses are general assumptions. They are very abstract, hypothetical but testable statements. In each and every hypothesis, there are independent and dependable variables. Hypotheses should also be in line with the objectives of the study. According to Mugenda and Mugenda (2003), hypothesis may be directional or non-directional and researchers are only able to state a directional hypothesis when some information on the phenomenon under study is available. Also, hypotheses may be substituted for research questions if the study is exploratory.

Theoretical or Conceptual Framework—A theoretical framework is applied when the research is not as complex and can be dealt with by the use of one theory to look at and/or analyse while a conceptual framework is best used when the researcher wants to get out of the box and look at different theories in order to borrow relevant elements from them or when one wants to conceptualise and build a model either by adopting from, or modifying an already existing concept.

Researchers can have either a theoretical framework or a conceptual framework, not both. Whichever the case, however, the researcher should also discuss the key tenets of the theory(s), various arguments put forth by the proponents as well as opponents of such theory(ies). It should also end with a paragraph on the relevance of the theory or conceptual framework and how it helps the researcher analyse his study.

In any case, theories are formulated to explain, predict, and understand phenomena and, in many cases, to challenge and extend existing knowledge within the limits of critical bounding assumptions. The theoretical framework is the structure that can hold or support a theory of a research study. The theoretical framework introduces and describes the theory that explains why the research problem under study exists (Abend, 2013).

Rationale or Justification of the Study—This section answers the question WHY? It follows from the background to persuade the reader that the study is needed and will be useful or interesting. Additionally, it may include reference to a 'gap' in the research literature, to the need to apply certain ideas in a new context, to the significance of this particular topic or the ways in which the study may be significant for the educational community may also be discussed. There are two (2) key questions that need to be answered here on the study's academic as well as policy relevance: In other words, how will this study contribute to the existing body of knowledge? How relevant is the study? For example, will it contribute to ongoing policy debates? This section seeks to justify the need for the study and how scholarship will benefit from it. Some citations can be done if/when found necessary.

Literature Review—This section shows the writer's supervisor and faculty that one is aware of significant scholars in the field and indicates which issues or topics one will focus on in their review. It also shows that one can be judicious in one's selection of issues to focus on and take an approach of critical inquiry and situate one's research within the field. This is not expected to be extensive for the proposal. One should conduct an initial survey of the main theories and a library information search to establish one's direction and formulate a tentative list of readings that can demonstrate a critical analysis. Their review should also be shaped by one's argument and should seek to establish his/her theoretical orientation.

This section is divided into sections and subsections. But, first, one should start with an introduction of what the literature review covers and then move onto its different sections and sub sections. It is supposed to provide a synthesis of the existing literature, with special focus on some specific areas, but in relation to the topic. The literature review is based on the number of variables that are in one's research topic. At the end, the literature review should have a section on a 'literature gap' which is meant to provide a brief assessment of the literature hence the identification of the gap within which the proposed study aims to fill. In this section, only academic books or sources are acceptable and no less than 23 to 43 books or other academic sources should be used.

Research Methodology—Decisions regarding what, where, when, how much, and by what means concerning an inquiry or a research study constitute a research design. Research design is the arrangement of conditions for collection and analysis of data in a manner that aims to combine relevance to the research purpose with economy in procedure (Selltiz, 1962). It contains the sampling design which deals with the method of selecting items to be observed for the given study; the observational design which relates to the conditions under which the observations are to be made; the statistical design which is concerned with the question of how many items are to be observed and how the information and data gathered are to be analysed; and the operational design which deals with the techniques by which the procedures specified in the sampling, statistical and observational designs can be carried out (Kothari, 2004).

Generally, the design which minimises bias and maximises the reliability of the data collected and analysed is considered a good design. The design which gives the smallest experimental error is supposed to be the best design in many investigations. Similarly, a design which yields maximum information and provides an opportunity for considering many different aspects of a problem is considered a most appropriate and efficient design in respect of many research problems. Thus, the question of a good design is related to the purpose or objective of the research problem and also to the nature of the problem to be studied (Kothari, 2004).

This section seeks to answer the question HOW? It includes one's understanding of the nature of knowledge and how this affects one's choice of research approach. It includes the description of and rationale for selection of participants, methods of data collection and analysis, procedures one will use to ensure ethical practice, validity and reliability and a statement about the delimitations (scope) of the study.

In no more than three (3) paragraphs, the researcher is required to explain how he/she will collect data: primary and secondary sources of information. He/she will then provide details of how they will use each of the proposed methodology, i.e. desk study and analysis, sample size, selection process etc. Then, he/she deals with the scope and limitation of the study.

Discussion, Conclusions and Recommendations—Discussions cover the critical review and comparison of one's own results with the literature review. An explanation of similarities or differences with empirical studies is expected. Broad conclusions based on the research objectives, analysis done and the results obtained should be covered. Recommendations are classified as "Suggestions for Improvement" on policy and management gaps and "Suggestions for further Research."

In this last section, a discussion of the suggestions for further research emerging from the scope, the methodology, unexpected findings and gaps left from the discussion of the results, and, of the study will also be covered.

References and Bibliography—This is a complete or selective list of information sources or works compiled upon some common principle, as authorship, subject, place of publication, or publisher. It can also be defined as a list of source materials that are used or consulted in the preparation of the work or that are referred to in the text. While references are those sources directly used, the bibliography covers all the sources whether used or not.

Conclusions

While there are many different ways to package a proposal, the above structure gives the best and the most balanced. However, one must take note that a good research proposal is a prerequisite and it leads to a good research output. In terms of writing up the research findings, a good report can be structured around the following:

a) Introduction/Background
b) Literature Review
c) Research Methodology
d) Discussion/Analysis of Data/Findings, and
e) Conclusions/Recommendations.

End of Chapter 10 Quiz

In this section, students, with the guidance of their lecturer, will pick a researchable topic and write up a draft research proposal which will be used as an examination of the 'Research Methodology' course. The research proposal MUST meet the criteria prescribed above. While doing so, also take consideration of everything you have learnt about research since Chapter 1.

RESEARCH ETHICS

> *"It is important to consider ethical issues from the early stages of a research project. From the beginning of the design process, provisional decisions are usually taken about the nature of the research sample, and of the methodology."*
>
> — **Paul Oliver (2010)**

Introduction

Ethics involves the attempt to formulate codes and principles of moral behaviour. That is, the capacity of ethical inquiry is to inform reasons for action (May, 2011). Social scientists, perhaps to a greater extent than the average citizen, have an ethical obligation to their colleagues, their study population, and the larger society. The reason for this is that social scientists delve into the social lives of other human beings. From such excursions into private social lives, various policies, practices, and even laws may result. Thus, researchers must ensure the rights, privacy and welfare of the people and communities that form the focus of their studies.

Research ethics is important because science has often been manipulated in unethical ways by people and organizations to advance their private agenda and engage in activities that are contrary to the norms of scientific conduct. Social researchers work within a variety of economic, cultural, legal and political settings, each of which influences the emphasis and focus of their research. They also work within one of several different branches of their discipline, each involving its own techniques and procedures and its own ethical approach. Many social researchers work in fields such as economics, psychology, sociology and medicine whose practitioners have ethical conventions that may influence the conduct of researchers and their fields. Even within the same setting and branch of social research, individuals may have different moral precepts that guide their work. Thus, no declaration could successfully impose a rigid set of rules to which social researchers everywhere should be expected to adhere, and this document does not attempt to do so.

Ethical Principles of Social Research Methods

Some of the expected tenets of ethical behaviour that are widely accepted within the scientific community are as follows:

a) *Voluntary participation and harmlessness:* Subjects in a research project must be aware that their participation in the study is voluntary, that they have the freedom to withdraw from the study at any time without any unfavourable consequences, and they are not harmed as a result of their participation or non-participation in the project.

b) *Anonymity and confidentiality:* To protect subjects' interests and future well-being, their identity must be protected in a scientific study. This is done using the dual principles of anonymity and confidentiality. Anonymity implies that the researcher or readers of the final research report or paper cannot identify a given response with a specific respondent.

c) *Disclosure:* Usually, researchers have an obligation to provide some information about their study to potential subjects before data collection, to help them decide whether or not they wish to participate in the study. For instance: Who is conducting the study? For what purpose? What outcomes are expected? And, who will benefit from the results? However, in some cases, disclosing such information may potentially bias subjects' responses.

d) *Analysis and reporting:* Researchers also have ethical obligations to the scientific community on how data is analysed and reported in their study. Unexpected or negative findings should be fully disclosed, even if they cast some doubt on the research design or the findings. Similarly, many interesting relationships are discovered after a study is completed, by chance or data mining. It is unethical to present such findings as the product of deliberate design.

Professional Codes of Ethics

Most professional associations of researchers have established and published formal codes of conduct describing what constitute *acceptable* and *unacceptable* professional behaviour of their member researchers. As an example, the summarized code of conduct for the Association of Information Systems (AIS), the global professional association of researchers in the information systems discipline, is summarized below. Similar codes of ethics are also available for other disciplines.

Category One: Codes in this category must **always** be adhered to and disregard for them constitutes a serious ethical breach. Serious breaches can result in your expulsion from academic associations, dismissal from your employment, legal action against you and potentially fatal damage to your academic reputation.

- Do not plagiarize.
- Do not fabricate or falsify data, research procedures or data analysis.

Category Two: Codes in this category are recommended ethical behaviour. Flagrant disregard of these codes or other kinds of professional etiquette, while less serious, can result in damage to your reputation, editorial sanctions, professional embarrassment, legal action, and the ill will of your colleagues.

a) Respect the rights of research subjects, particularly their rights to information privacy, and to being informed about the nature of the research and the types of activities in which they will be asked to engage.

b) Do not make misrepresentations to editors and conference programme chairs about the originality of papers you submit to them.

c) Do not abuse the authority and responsibility you have been given as an editor, reviewer or supervisor, and ensure that personal relationships do not interfere with your judgment.

d) Declare any material conflict of interest that might interfere with your ability to be objective and impartial when reviewing submissions, grant applications, software, or undertaking work from outsidesources.

e) Do not take or use published data of others without acknowledgement, or unpublished data without both permission and acknowledgement.

f) Acknowledge the substantive contributions of all research participants, whether colleagues or students, according to their intellectual contribution.

g) Do not use other people's unpublished writings, information, ideas, concepts or data that you may see as a result of processes such as peer review without permission of the author.

h) Use archival material only in accordance with the rules of the archival source.

i) Always protect yourself from authorship disputes, mis-steps, mistakes, and even legal action.

j) Keep the documentation and data necessary to validate your original authorship for each scholarly work with which you are connected.

k) Do not republish old ideas of your own as if they were a new intellectual contribution.

l) Settle data set ownership issues before data compilation.

m) Consult appropriate colleagues if in doubt.

n) Always focus to generate new knowledge.

Codes and Policies for Research Ethics

Given the importance of ethics for the conduct of research, it should come as no surprise that many different professional associations, government agencies and universities have adopted specific codes, rules, and policies relating to research ethics. The following is a general summary of some ethical principles that various codes address:

a) Honesty: Strive for honesty in all scientific communications. Honestly report data, results, methods and procedures, and publication status. Do not fabricate, falsify, or misrepresent data. Do not deceive colleagues, research sponsors, or the public.

b) Objectivity: Strive to avoid bias in experimental design, data analysis, data interpretation, peer review, personnel decisions, grant writing, expert testimony, and other aspects of research where objectivity is expected or required. Avoid or minimize bias or self-deception. Disclose personal or financial interests that may affect research.

c) Integrity: Keep your promises and agreements; act with sincerity; strive for consistency of thought and action.

d) Carefulness: Avoid careless errors and negligence; carefully and critically examine your own work and the work of your peers. Keep good records of research activities, such as data collection, research design, and correspondence with agencies or journals.

e) Openness: Share data, results, ideas, tools, resources. Be open to criticism and new ideas.

f) Respect for Intellectual Property: Honor patents, copyrights, and other forms of intellectual property. Do not use unpublished data, methods, or results without permission. Give proper acknowledgement or credit for all contributions to research. Never plagiarize.

g) Confidentiality: Protect confidential communications such as papers or grants submitted for publication, personnel records, trade or military secrets, and patient records.

h) Responsible Publication: Publish in order to advance research and scholarship, not to advance just your own career. Avoid wasteful and duplicative publication.

i) Responsible Mentoring: Help to educate, mentor, and advise students. Promote their welfare and allow them to make their own decisions.

j) Respect for Colleagues: Respect your colleagues and treat them fairly.

k) Social Responsibility: Strive to promote the social good and prevent or mitigate social harms through research, public education, and advocacy.

l) Non-Discrimination: Avoid discrimination against colleagues or students on the basis of sex, race, ethnicity, or other factors not related to scientific competence and integrity.

m) Competence: Maintain and improve your own professional competence and expertise through lifelong education and learning; take steps to promote competence in science as a whole.

n) Legality: Know and obey relevant laws and institutional and governmental policies.

o) Animal Care: Show proper respect and care for animals when using them in research. Do not conduct unnecessary or poorly designed animal experiments.

p) Human Subjects Protection: When conducting research on human subjects, minimise harms and risks and maximise benefits; respect human dignity, privacy, and autonomy; take special precautions with vulnerable populations; and strive to distribute the benefits and burdens of research fairly.

q) Policy Orientation: Once research done and is officially filed, scholars need to redevelop their papers and turn them into policy briefs, chapters in books and valuable articles in refereed journals; hence the need to contribute not only to the existing body of knowledge but also to ongoing policy debates in their fields. If any, this is a major contribution to humanity.

Plagiarism

According to the American Association of University Professors, plagiarism is defined as: "Taking over the ideas, methods, or written words of another, without acknowledgment and with the intention that they be taken as the work of the deceiver."(Bergan, et al. 2020).

As the above quotation states, plagiarism has been traditionally defined as the taking of words, images, ideas, etc., from an author and presenting them as one's own. It is often associated with phrases, such as kidnapping of words, kidnapping of ideas, fraud and literary theft.

Plagiarism can manifest itself in a variety of ways and it is not just confined to student papers or published articles or books. For example, consider a scientist who makes a presentation at a conference and discusses at length an idea or concept that had already been proposed by someone else and that is not considered common knowledge. During his presentation, he fails to fully acknowledge the specific source of the idea and, consequently, misleads the audience into thinking that he was the originator of that idea. This, too, may constitute an instance of plagiarism. In sum, plagiarism can be a very serious form of ethical misconduct. For this reason, the concept of plagiarism is universally addressed in all scholarly, artistic, and scientific disciplines.

Referencing

A reference gives full details of the source cited in the work; the parts or elements of the reference should be noted in a consistent order. Use of a recognized style guide will help ensure consistency, and will also ensure that all required elements are included. If we fail to show that we are using someone else's words, work or ideas by not indicating that they originated with someone else, then we mislead the reader. If we give the impression that these words or ideas are our own when they are not, this is not good scholarship and, whether deliberate or unintentional, may be deemed as academic misconduct.

This document provides guidance on referencing and demonstrates some of the differences between the most widely used styles. As a student, it is important that you identify in your assessment when you are using the words or ideas of another author. The most accepted way of acknowledging the work of another author is to use a referencing system.

As a part of an academic community, it is important that you show the reader where you have used someone else's ideas or words. Failure to properly reference using a recognized style of documentation may make the reader think that you are cheating by claiming someone else's work as your own.

In the academic environment, we call this *plagiarism* and it is seen as a very serious offence. Please remember that plagiarism is not just when you directly copy words from another student's or expert's work. Plagiarism also occurs when you paraphrase someone else's ideas in your own work and you do not give credit to the original source.

On a more positive note, referencing is important for reasons other than avoiding plagiarism. When you reference correctly, you are demonstrating that you have read widely on a topic. You are also supporting your hypothesis with comments from expert authors. This lends credibility to your own work. Also, by correctly referencing, you allow the marker or reader to follow-up your references and to check the validity of your arguments for themselves. This is an important part of the academic process as it leads to student accountability.

Style Guide

A *style guide* is a published manual that gives guidance on citation and references to help ensure that our documentation is expressed consistently, and that we include all the elements needed for our sources to be identified. Some style guides offer more than one set of choices or sub-styles; if we use a particular sub-style, we must be sure to use the same sub-style throughout our work. As well as advice on citations and referencing, many published style guides give advice on *spelling, abbreviations, punctuations,* and so on.

Many also give guidance on research and the general writing process. Style guides in common use in the academic world include the following:

a) **MLA (Modern Language Association).** The MLA style is a system for documenting sources in scholarly writing. For over half a century, it has been widely adopted for classroom instruction and used worldwide by scholars, journal publishers, and academic and commercial presses. When using MLA style, writers place references to sources in the paper to briefly identify them and enable readers to find them in the Works Cited List.

Format: Author Last, First. *Title*. Location of Publisher: Publisher, Year of Publication.

Sample Citation: Welch, Kathleen. *Electric Rhetoric*. Cambridge: MIT Press. 1999.

b) **APA (American Psychological Association).** The APA style requires that sources receive attribution in the text by the use of parenthetical in-text references.

Format: Author Last, First Initial. (Year of Publication). *Title*. Publisher Location: Publisher.

Sample Citation: Welch, K.E. (1999). *Electric rhetoric: Classical rhetoric, oralism, and a new literacy*. Cambridge: MIT Press.

Please **NOTE:** This is the preferred style in the 21st Century academic world.

c) **Harvard is a style of referencing**, primarily used by university students, to cite information sources. Harvard Reference List citations follow this format: **Format:** Last name, First Initial. (Year published). *Title*. City: Publisher, Page(s). Citations are listed in alphabetical order by the author's last name. If there are multiple sources by the same author, then citations are listed in order by the date of publication.

d) **Chicago or Turabian:** Chicago referencing style is a widely used referencing system. The Chicago style involves two tasks: How you reference sources through numbered footnote or endnote citation as opposed to in-text citation. How you compile a list of reference sources at the end of your text (reference list).

Note that local variations between style guides exist and writers should be sure to follow a single style guide consistently. When consulted sources are accessed online, there is preference to use Uniform Resource Locators (URLs) or Digital Object Identifiers (DOIs), even if the published style guide makes them optional.

Research Ethics and Law

Ethical principles in any profession are based on the understanding that members of associations will abide by the principles. Unfortunately, this is not often the case and many researchers and/or institutions have breached ethical codes in furtherance of sinister motives. As such, researchers are also bound by relevant local and international laws as an enforcement mechanism for ethical principles. Whereas legal provisions are always broad, covering any type of ethical breaches, voluntary participation, disclosure, confidentiality, falsification of data and plagiarism are the areas in which researchers as well as other institutions, educational or otherwise, have often faced legal consequences for breach of ethical principles.

Conclusions

It is important to adhere to ethics while conducting research. Equally important is also the need to reference information by borrowing ideas – and not stealing – from other scholars. Ethical lapses in research often have a tremendous effect on science and society in general. It does compromise the integrity of research by eroding public trust. It also leads to a waste of time, energy and other resources. Research ethics, and proper referencing, will significantly reduce instances of misconduct in research, it will sensitize researchers about ethical issues, and practically teach them ethical dilemmas and other related issues that they may face while undertaking research.

End of Chapter 11 Quiz

a) Briefly discuss the importance of anonymity and confidentiality as an ethical principle of research.

b) Take an academic environment where **plagiarism** is condoned. What would be some of the main ramifications?

c) In groups, propose and discuss 3-5 measures that can prevent falsification of research data in academic environments.

d) In groups, read about the Tuskegee Experiment and the case between Henrietta Lacks and Johns Hopkins University and discuss the ethical principles breached.

e) What is the relationship between ethics and law?

Pre-Exam Review

In this section, students shall go through and review the whole syllabus. With emphasis on the more practical sessions, it is meant to serve as a pre- exam review on all the topics covered. Students are, therefore, advised to engage in more lively and interactive discussions. The session shall also have a site visit or a study tour in which students shall pay a visit to either a think- tank (University campus), and/or a field project site where they can have the opportunity to test some of their research skills. Finally, the session shall end with a class discussion of a summary of the key messages from the course.

ANNEX 01
TRAINING OF TRAINERS (TOT)

This section deals with how to train the trainers. It is about the necessary skills that those engaged in the training of adults require. The philosophy of the ToT curriculum is based on three principles: First, adults learn what they want and when they want it; second, nobody knows everything but everybody knows something; and third and last, learning is a process. It is divided into two sub-sections:

- Adult Learning Techniques & Methodologies (the ALTEM[1] concept); and

- Course Methodology.

---

1 This concept was tested with the help of a number of people and institutions including Mr. Abdirashid Adan Ibrahim, former Head of Civilian Component, Eastern Africa Standby Force (EASF), Gen. Charles Wacha, Head of Human Rights Unit, Uganda Peoples Defense Forces (UPDF), Mr. Simiyu Werunga and Mr. John Haguma who were fellow course facilitators at the International Peace Support Training Institute (IPSTC) and the Rwanda Peace Academy (RPA) respectively on a number of courses related to Peacekeeping (and Peace Support) Operations (PKOs/PSOs) at various sessions in Somalia, Kenya, Uganda, Rwanda and Ethiopia. The concept was also tested, under the leadership of Prof. Farah, at the AMIC 2014, an EASF exercise with which EASF's Full Operational Capability (FOC) was realised in late 2014 in Adama, Ethiopia. We are deeply grateful to all; both the said individual figures as well as the EASF, the IPSTC and the RPA for their institutional roles in having the ALTEM concept tested through course deliveries.

Adult Learning Techniques and Methodologies (ALTEM)

Introduction

According to Lieb (1991), part of being an effective trainer involves some knowledge of how adults learn best. Andragogy—adult learning—is a theory that holds a set of assumptions about how adults learn. It emphasises the value of the *process* of learning. It uses pedagogical approaches to learning that are *problem-based* and *collaborative* rather than didactic or instructive; and it also emphasises more *equality* between the lecturer or teacher and the learner.

'Andragogy' as a study of adult learning originated in Europe in the 1950s and was then pioneered as a theory and model of adult learning from the 1970s by Malcolm Knowles, an American practitioner and theorist of adult education, who defined andragogy as 'the art and science of helping adults learn (Zmeyov, 1998; Fidishun, 2000).

Adult Learning Principles

Knowles (1980) identified six (6) key principles of adult learning: i) Internal motivation and self-direction; ii) From life experiences and knowledge to learning experiences; iii) Goal-orientation; iv) Relevance; v) Practicality; and vi) Respect. In addition, the link of the concept of 'Rationality, Creativity & Critical thinking (RCC) with goal-orientation is also equally important; hence seven (7) principles.

The ALTEM concept: Marrying theory with practice

1) Internal motivation & Self-direction

Adult learners resist learning when they feel others are imposing information, ideas or actions on them (Fidishun, 2000). Trainers of adults therefore need to play the role of a facilitator and not an imposer. This is based on the fact that adults are internally-motivated and self-directed. In other words, they are like the person training them, and as a trainer, one can:

- Set up a graded learning programme that moves from more to less structure, from less to more responsibility and from more to less direct supervision, at an appropriate pace that is challenging yet not overloading for the learners.

- Develop rapport with the students in order to optimize one's approachability as the trainer encourages them to ask questions and explore concepts and options.

- Show interest in their thoughts and opinions by actively and carefully listening to any questions they ask.

- Lead the students toward inquiry before supplying them with too many facts.

- Provide regular constructive and specific feedback (both positive and negative).

- While providing negative feedback, lenient language and tone is desirable.

- Review goals and acknowledge goal completion.

- Encourage use of resources such as library, journals, internet and other relevant resources.

- Set projects or tasks that reflect their interests and which they must complete and 'tick-off' before the next session.

- Acknowledge their preferred learning style.

2) From life experiences & knowledge to learning experiences

Adults like to be given an opportunity to use their existing foundation of knowledge and experiences gained from life experience so that they may apply it to their new learning experiences. The trainer therefore can:

- Find out about your students' interests and past experiences.

- Assist them to draw on those experiences when problem-solving, reflecting, and/or applying logic and reasoning processes.

- Facilitate reflective learning opportunities which, according to Fidishun (2000), can also assist students to examine existing biases or habits based on life experiences and move them toward a new understanding of the information presented.

3) Goal-orientation

According to Knowles (1980), adults become ready to learn when they experience a need to learn it in order to cope more satisfactorily with real-life tasks or problems. Your role as a trainer is, therefore, to facilitate their readiness for problem-based learning and help them increase their awareness of the need for the knowledge or the skill presented. A trainer can thus:

- Provide meaningful learning experiences that are clearly linked to their goals, be they personal, client, fieldwork or group goals.

- Provide real case-studies as a basis from which to learn theory and marry it with practice, be they issues of methodology, significance, implications of relevance.

- Ask questions that motivate reflection, inquiry and further research.

4) Relevance

Adults want to know the relevance of what they are learning to what they want to achieve. As a trainer, one has the responsibility of helping them see the value of their observations and practical experiences throughout the programme/ course. The trainer therefore has to:

- Ask them to do some reflections on their expectations and how they might apply the new knowledge gained from the programme or course, in future, and/or how it will help them meet their learning goals.

- Provide some choice of fieldwork projects by providing two or more options, so that learning is more likely to reflect their interests.

- Engage them in the selection process and research programme development from the outset of the training course.

5) Practicality

Through practical fieldwork experiences, interacting with real clients and their real-life situations, adults like to move from classroom and textbook mode to hands-on problem-solving models. The hands-on approaches provide them with first hand opportunity to recognize how what they are learning applies to their life and work context. The trainer thus can:

- Clearly explain your logic and reasoning when making choices about assessments, interventions and when prioritising needs.

- Be explicit about how useful what they are learning is as well as its applicability to the job market.

- Promote active participation by allowing them to try things rather than limit them to only observation.

6) Respect

As a trainer, one can demonstrate respect to students by:

- Taking interest in what they are doing and regarding them as colleagues who are equals in life experience.

- Acknowledging the wealth of experiences that they bring to the class.

- Encouraging expression of ideas, reasoning and feedback at every opportunity possible.

7) Rationality, creativity & critical thinking to goal-orientation

As a trainer, there are two general tips that may also be helpful while designing TOT programmes for adult learners:

- Trainers need to apply the Rationality, Creativity and Critical thinking (RCC) model throughout. The RCC model tends to marry theory with practice; thereby boosting interest.

- Adopt goal-orientation as the first priority, the second priority and the third priority; and finally,

- Always move with your independence, traditions and values!

Course Methodology[2]

The following are the recommended course methods:

- Lecture Seminars and Group Work Discussions
- Case/Comparative Studies
- Critique of Journal Articles or Book Reviews
- Guest Lectures (Mainly from a practitioner's perspective)
- Site Visits (to research institutions, Universities and other think-tanks)
- Field-work (by the students to test their data collection and analysis skills)
- Essays, research papers or articles & peer reviews (for each other's works).

---

2 This kind of interactive methodology must be supported by a reading list, preferably non-exhaustive, with which students must be encouraged to go beyond and read widely.

Bibliography

Abend, Gabriel. "The Meaning of Theory." *Sociological Theory* 26 (June 2008): 173–199.

ACAPS (2012) *Qualitative and Quantitative Research Techniques for Humanitarian Needs Assessment.*

Ackoff L. (1961), *The Design of Social Research*, Chicago University Press, Chicago.

Aliaga, M., & Gunderson, B. (2000). *Interactive Statistics*. Upper Saddle River, NJ: Prentice Hall.

Angen, M.J., *Evaluating interpretive inquiry: Reviewing the validity debate and opening the dialogue. Qualitative Health Research.* 10(3) pp. 378-395., 2000.

Anol Bhattacherjee, "Social Science Research: Principles, Methods, and Practices." *Textbooks Collection*. 3., 2012.

Anthony J. Onwuegbuzie, "Writing a Research Proposal: The Role of Library Anxiety, Statistics Anxiety, and Composition Anxiety", *Library & Information Science Research*, Vol. 19, No. 1, pp. 5-33, 1997.

Babbie, E. (1998). *The Practice of Social Research* (8th ed). Belmont, CA: Wadsworth Publishing.

Balnaves, M & Caputi, P. (2001). *Introduction to Quantitative Research*

Methods: An Investigative Approach. Sage Publication. New Delhi, India.

Bellenger D., and Barnett, A., (2014). *Marketing Research—A Management Information Approach.* RD Irwin.

Berg. B. L., & Berg, J., "A re-examination of triangulation and objectivity in qualitative nursing research." *Free Inquiry in Creative Sociology* 21(1), 65-72, 1993.

Biemer, Paul, and Lars Lyberg. (2003). *Introduction to Survey Quality.* Hoboken, NJ: John Wiley & Sons.

Blalock, H & Blalock (Eds) (1968). *Methods in Social Science Research,* New York, McGrew Hill.

Blanchard P., "A Psycho-Analytic Study of Auguste Comte", *The American Journal of Psychology,* Vol. 29, No.2, University of Illinois Press, 1918.

Blumer, M. (1984). *The Chicago School of Sociology: Institutionalization, Diversity, and the Rise of Sociological Research.* Chicago: University of Chicago Press.

Bryman, A. (2001). *Social Research Methods.* Oxford University Press, Oxford.

Cohen L., Manion L., and Morrison K. (2007), *Research Methods in Education,* (6th ed) New York, USA, Rutledge.

Creswell, John W. (2009). *Research Design: Qualitative, Quantitative, and Mixed Methods Approaches. 3rd Edition.* Los Angeles: Sage Publications, Inc.

Creswell, John W. (2015), *A Concise Introduction to Mixed Methods Approach,* SAGE Publications Inc.

Creswell, J. W., & Clark, V. L. P. (2007). *Designing and conducting mixed methods research.* Sage Publications, Inc.

Creswell, J. W. (2014). *Research Design: Qualitative, Quantitative and* Mixed Methods Approaches (4th ed.). Thousand Oaks, CA: Sage.

Clifford W., The Values of Educational Research to the Classroom Teacher, The Journal of Educational Research, *Volume 16, Issue 3, 1927.*

Collins, H. (2010). *Creative Research: The Theory and Practice of Research for the Creative Industries.* Singapore: AVA Publications.

Crothers C. and Platt J., "The History and Development of Sociological Social Research Methods", *Historical Developments and Theoretical Approaches in Sociology, Vol. 1, Encyclopedia of Life Support Systems,* 2003.

Crotty, M. (2003). *The Foundation of Social Research: Meaning and Perspective in the Research Process.* Thousand Oaks, CA: Sage.

Denscombe M. (2004), *The Good Research Guide for Small Scale Social Research,* 2nd Edition, Open University Press.

Denzin, Norman K.; Lincoln, Yvonna S. (1998), *The Landscape of Qualitative Research: Theories and Issues,* Sage Publications, Inc.

Donatella Della Porta and Michael Keating, (2008). Approaches and methodologies in social sciences: a pluralist perspective. Cambridge University Press, Cambridge, New York,

Don A. Dillman, (2003). "The Design and Administration of Mail Surveys," *Annual Review of Sociology* 17(1):225-249

Dudwick, N., Kuehnast, K., Jones, V. N., and Woolcock, M. (2006), *Analyzing Social Capital in Context: A Guide to Using Qualitative Methods and Data,* World Bank Institute, Washington.

Edith D. de Leeuw, "To Mix or Not to Mix Data Collection Modes in Surveys," *Journal of Official Statistics,* Vol. 21, No. 2, 2005, pp. 233-255.

Fidishun, Dolores. "Andragogy and Technology: Integrating Adult

Learning Theory as We Teach with Technology," *5th Annual Instructional Technology Conference*, April 9-11, 2000, Middle Tennessee State University.

Frankfort-*Nachmias*, C. and *Nachmias*, D. (2000). *Research Methods in the Social Sciences*. 6th Edition, Wadsworth, New York.

Freitas, H., Oliveira, M., Jenkins, M., & Popjoy, O. (1998). *The Focus Group: A Qualitative Research Method*. ISRC, Merrick School of Business.

Given Lisa (2008), *The Sage Encyclopedia of Research Methods*, Los Angeles, California.

Glaser, B., & Strauss, A. (1967). *The Discovery of Grounded Theory: Strategies for Qualitative Research*. Mill Valley, CA: Sociology Press.

Glassner, B., Ksander, M., Johnson, B., & Berg, B. L. (1983). "The deterrence effect of juvenile versus adult jurisdiction." *Social Problems 32 (2)*, 219-221.

Gorard S. (2003). *The role of numbers in social science research: quantitative methods made easy*, London: Continuum.

Groves R. "Theories and methods of telephone surveys." *Annual Review of Sociology*. 1990; 16:221–240.

Hallebone, E. and Priest, J. (2009), *Business. and Management Research: Paradigms and Practices*, Palgrave Macmillan, New York.

Holier Collins (2011), *Creative Research the Theory and Practice of Research for the Creative Industry*, AVA Publications.

Howard S. Becker (1970), Sociological Work, Chica. Aldine Publishing Co.

Jick, T.D. (1979). "Mixing Qualitative and Quantitative Methods: Triangulation in Action Mixing Qualitative and Quantitative

Methods: Triangulation in Action." *Administrative Science Quarterly*, 24, 602-611.

Johnny Saldana, (2011), *Fundamentals of Qualitative Research: Understanding Qualitative Research*, Oxford University Press.

Johnson, B. and Turner, L.A. (2003) "Data Collection Strategies in Mixed Methods Research." In: Tashakkori, A.M. and Teddlie, C.B., Eds., *Handbook of Mixed Methods in Social and Behavioral Research*, SAGE Publications, Thousand Oaks, 297-319.

Johnson R. B. & Christensen, L. B. (2011). *Educational Research: Quantitative, Qualitative, and Mixed Approaches*, Fourth edition. SAGE Publications, Inc. LA, USA.

Johnson R. B and Onwegbuzie A.J. "Mixed Methods Research: A Paradigm whose Time has come?" *Educational Researcher*, 33 (7), 2014. Sage international (P) Limited.

Julian Henriques, Wendy Hollay, Cathy Urwin, Couze Venn, Valerie Walkerdine (1998), *Changing the Subject: Psychology, Social Regulation and Subjectivity*. Routledge.

Kincaid H. (1998), *Positivism in the Social Sciences: Encyclopedia of Philosophy*, Rutledge, London.

Kothari C.R., *Research Methodology: Methods and Techniques (2nd ed.)*, New Age International Publishers, 2004.

Knowles, M. S. (1980). *The Modern Practice of Adult Education: From Pedagogy to Andragogy* (revised and updated). Englewood Cliffs, NJ: Cambridge Adult Education.

Lee, R M. (1993). *Doing Research on &Sensitive Topics*. Newbury Park, CA: Sage.

Lieb, S. (1991). *Principles of Adult Learning*. Phoenix, AZ: Vision-South Mountain Community College.

MacDonald, S. & Headlam N. (2015). *Research Methods Handbook:*

Introductory Guide to Research Methods for Social Research. Manchester: Centre for Local Economic Strategies.

Macionis John and Gerber Linda (2010), *Sociology Seventh Canadian Edition*, Pearson, Canada.

Mansfield, Y. "From Motivation to Actual Travel." *Annals of Tourism Research.* 19: 399- 419. 1992.

Meir, Robert C., Newell, William T., and Dazier, Harold L. (1969), *Simulation in Business and Economics*, Englewood Cliffs, N.J: Prentice Hall, Inc.

Michael H. Agar (1980). *The professional stranger: An informal introduction to ethnography*. New York: Academic Press.

Mishra, Shanti B and Shashi Alok (2012) *A Handbook of Research Methodology: A Compendium for Scholars and Researchers.* New Delhi: Educreation Publishing.

Muijs, D. (2004). *Doing Quantitative Research in Education with SPSS.* London; Thousand Oaks, CA; New Delhi: Sage Publications.

Mutchnick, R. J. and B. L. Berg. (1996), *Research Methods for the Social Sciences: Practice and Applications.* Boston: Allyn and Bacon.

Nilson, K., "Where industry meets nature. How public concern has influenced the design of Swedish industrial landscapes during the 20th century." *Landscape and Urban planning* 23:1, 33-45., 1992.

Olive M. Mugenda and Abel G. Mugenda, (2003). *Research Methods: Quantitative and Qualitative Approaches*, Nairobi: ACTS Press.

Orlikowski, W. J. "Integrated Information Environment or Matrix of Control? The Contradictory Implications of Information Technology," *Accounting, Management and Information Technologies* (1:1), 1991, pp. 9-42.

Owen E. Hughes (2012), *Public Management & Administration: An Introduction*, 4th Edition, PALGRAVE MACMILLAN.

Patton, M. Q. (1990). *Qualitative evaluation and research methods* (2nd ed.). Sage Publications, Inc.

Paul Oliver (2010), *The Student's Guide to Research Ethics*, 2nd Edition, McGraw-Hill Open University Press.

Paul R. Rosenbaum (2005). "An Exact Distribution-Free Test Comparing Two Multivariate Distributions Based on Adjacency." *Journal of the Royal Statistical Society Series B* (Statistical Methodology) 67(4):515-530.

Polit, Denise F. and Cheryl Tatano, Beck, *Nursing Research: Generating and Assessing Evidence for Nursing Practice*. Philadelphia, Wolters Kluwer, 2010.

Ryan, Anne B. (2006) *"Post-Positivist Approaches to Research."* In: Researching and Writing your thesis: a guide for postgraduate students. MACE: Maynooth Adult and Community Education, pp. 12-26.

Ritchie J.E., and Lewis J.E., (ed.). (2003), *Qualitative Research Practice: A Guide for Social Science Students and Researchers*, London, Sage Publications.

Schartz M., and Walker R. (1995), *Research as a Social Change*, Routledge.

Selltiz, Claire: Jahoda, Marie, Deutsch, Morton, and Cook, Stuart W. (1959), *Research Methods in Social Relations*, rev. ed. New York: Holt, Rinehart and Winston, Inc.

Shuttleworth Martyn, *Validity and Reliability*, October 20, 2008. Retrieved from https://explorable.com/validity-and-reliability accessed on 25 September 2015.

Sjur Bergan, Tony Gallagher and Ira Harkavy (eds). (2020), Academic freedom, institutional autonomy and the future of democracy (*Council of Europe Higher Education Series No. 24*).

Suphat Sukamolsom (2007). "Fundamentals of Quantitative Research." *Language Institute Chulalongkorn University*, 1: 2-3.

Tashakkori, A., & Teddlie, C. (1998). *Mixed methodology: Combining qualitative and quantitative approaches.* Sage Publications, Inc.

Tennis J., "Epistemology, Theory, and Methodology in Knowledge Organization: Toward a Classification, Metatheory, and Research Framework," *The Information School of the University of Washington, In Knowledge Organization*, 35(2/3): 102-112, 2008.

Timothy Williamson, "How did we get here from there? The transformation of analytic philosophy." *Belgrade Philosophical Annual* 27:7-37 (2014).

Weitzman, E. A. (2000). "Software and qualitative research." In N. Denzin and Y. Lincoln (Eds.) *Handbook of qualitative research*, 2nd Ed (pp. 803-820). Thousand Oaks, CA: Sage.

Wellington, J., Hunt, C., McCulloch, G. & Sikes, P. (2005). *Succeeding with Your Doctorate*. California: Sage

Yauch, C. A. and Steudel, H. J. (2003) "Complementary Use of Qualitative and Quantitative Cultural Assessment Methods," *Organizational Research Methods*, Vol. 6, No. 4.

Zmeyov, S. I. (1998). "Andragogy: Origins, developments and trends." *International Review Education*, 44(1), 103-108.

Index

A
analytical techniques 9
applied research 3, 104
arbitrary 77
attitude 46, 74
authoritarian knowledge 28

B
behavioural phenomena 32
bivariate 76, 89
blueprint 65, 66

C
causal relationship between variables 2, 68, 103
codes of ethics 115
coding 15, 16, 89, 90, 96, 100
concept of phenomenalism 32
conceptual xi, xvi, 13, 65, 97, 104, 108
constructs 47, 48
convenience sample 49
correlation analysis 33

D
data analysis 15, 16, 25, 40, 43, 47, 60, 76, 89, 90, 91, 96, 98, 99, 101, 102, 115, 117
dependent variable 69, 71, 74, 81, 88, 94
dependent variables 74, 94, 106
descriptive research 2, 71, 103, 104
descriptive studies 2, 68
descriptive tools 31
diagnostic research 2, 5, 70, 71, 103

E
empirical knowledge 28
empirical research 24, 104, 105
epistemology 27, 30, 48, 58
ethical scrutiny 35
ethical validity 30
ex post facto 2, 104
external validity 17, 33, 105
extraneous 69, 71, 75, 82, 88
extraneous variable 69, 71, 88

F
field of inquiry 21
findings ix, xi, 10, 16, 28, 32, 34, 35, 42, 46, 47, 49, 54, 58, 59, 60, 61, 62, 89, 98, 101, 106, 111, 112, 114, 115
focus group 8, 83
formulation of a research 11, 12

formulative research 1, 70, 103
frequency 2, 6, 13, 19, 45, 70, 75, 103, 104
fundamental research 3, 104

G

generalizability 33, 50, 60, 62

H

historical development of research methods 21
hypothesis 1, 2, 4, 6, 11, 12, 13, 15, 31, 33, 34, 40, 44, 65, 68, 69, 70, 71, 89, 91, 103, 105, 108, 120
hypothesis-testing 2, 68, 70, 103
hypothetical 4, 6, 106, 108

I

independent variable 68, 69, 71, 74, 81, 88, 94
inductive theory construction 47
inductive thinking 8
inferences 15, 58, 68, 71, 73, 90, 91
inferential 7, 43, 77, 89, 90
inherent capacity for repeatability 34
inquiry 1, 8, 11, 18, 21, 27, 30, 38, 57, 59, 64, 65, 109, 110, 113, 127, 128, 131
internal validity 33
interpretivism 25, 28, 36
interval 76, 77, 88, 91
interviewee 79
interviewer 79, 82

L

latitude 6
linguistic xvi, 85
literature review 28, 96, 97, 106, 109, 110, 111

logical knowledge 28
longitudinal research 5

M

mathematically based methods 37, 38
mean 9, 10, 33, 49, 91, 92, 93
mean deviation 92
measures of central tendency 75, 91, 92, 94
measures of dispersion 75, 91, 92, 94
median 33, 91, 92
meta-descriptive account of reality 31
mode 33, 34, 91, 92, 129
multivariate 76

N

non-probabilistic sample 14

O

observable phenomena 24, 32
organization of knowledge 27
outcome 90, 94

P

paradigm 24, 29, 38, 63
phenomenon 1, 2, 3, 6, 13, 19, 21, 33, 38, 46, 51, 55, 59, 64, 68, 88, 103, 104, 108
philosophical assumptions 57
plagiarism 119, 120, 122, 123
population 7, 14, 42, 46, 47, 50, 53, 55, 59, 71, 73, 74, 75, 83, 84, 86, 89, 91, 113
positivism theory 24
pragmatism 58
predetermined instruments 38
primary data 5, 15, 18, 28, 30, 73, 78, 87
probability sampling 42, 49, 50

purposive sample 50

Q

qualitative phenomena 3
quantitative evaluation 18
quantitative social research 40

R

range 44, 48, 61, 62, 83, 84, 85
ratio 76, 77, 88, 91
regression analysis 33, 43, 94
relativist ontology 30
reliability 14, 16, 31, 33, 44, 67, 68, 71, 91, 110, 111, 137
research ethics 117
research problem 10, 11, 12, 13, 23, 44, 57, 58, 60, 65, 68, 70, 87, 106, 107, 109, 110
research process 10, 11, 12, 15, 29, 30, 57

S

sample design 10, 11, 14, 66, 68
sampling 14, 42, 46, 49, 50, 55, 66, 72, 93, 110
scientific community 34, 114

secondary data 73, 96
sequential explanatory design 60
simulation approaches 7
smallest experimental error 67, 110
snowball sampling 50
social research settings 39
standard deviation 92
standard questionnaire 41
statistical calculations 38
statistical inferences 15
stratum 50
structured questionnaires 15
substantive validity 30
survey 7, 15, 18, 41, 42, 43, 44, 52, 68, 78, 79, 80, 104, 109

T

the conceptual structure 13, 65
triangulating data 59

U

univariate 89, 91, 92

V

validity 16, 17, 30, 33, 40, 44, 59, 89, 105, 111, 120, 131, 137